Praise for

IT'S ~~NOT~~ PERSONAL

"This has been the absent book in all the writing of church planting and pastoring. I highly recommend this for every young pastor
and church planter but require it for NorthWood church planters.
What makes church planting so hard for young men is that they
aren't just starting a church; most are starting a family. If we can't
have a healthy family, what difference does it make how big our
church is? If we can't model healthy homes, what does that say
about our message and leadership? I know Brian and Amy, and
they practice what they write."

— BOB ROBERTS JR.

"Finally a book for those who are on the front lines of ministry.
Brian and Amy nail the temptations, challenges, and best practices in the realm of church planting. They have stepped on the
landmines so that you don't have to. Read and heed their wisdom."

— PASTOR DARRIN PATRICK
Author of *For the City* and *Church Planter*

"Brian and Amy tell the story of church planting, and they tell
it like it is. So for everyone planning to plant a church, this is not
a book about principles, methods, or organization; get that elsewhere. This is about Brian, Amy, and you; it is about what will
happen to you and in you. This book is a must for anyone connected to church planting, because Brian and Amy make the task
so personal and triumphant. Read .... rejoice ... weep a little ...
and pray for the grace of God that was given to Brian and Amy
Bloye."

— ELMER L. TOWNS
Co-founder of Liberty University

"*It's Personal* by Brian and Amy Bloye offers so much wisdom that is needed to survive the church planting journey. What I love most is that they constantly point you back to Jesus to get the faith, wisdom, and perseverance to truly thrive personally while enjoying perhaps the biggest risk you'll ever take: planting a church."

—DAVE FERGUSON
Lead Pastor, Community Christian Church,
Movement Leader, NewThing

"If you are a church planter or are considering planting in the future, you need to read this book. I've personally watched Brian and Amy Bloye walk through many of the stories they share. Their candid reflections on their journey will challenge and inspire you."

—TONY MORGAN
Pastor, author, consultant

"Brian and Amy give church planters a real and raw look at what it takes to plant a church. This book is filled with encouraging, challenging, and practical stories that will give every church-planting couple the wisdom they need to navigate their own journey. The book had such a powerful impact on Cindy and me that we are making it required reading for every church planter that goes through the Launch Network training."

—MAC LAKE
LAUNCH Church Planting Network

"Church planting might just be the hardest job in ministry. It takes patience, courage, and an intense desire to take the message of the Gospel to hurting people. My friends Brian and Amy Bloye know exactly what that is like. *It's Personal* is an indispensible guide for anyone who is considering planting a church."

—GREG SURRATT
Lead Pastor, Seacoast Church,
and Author of *Ir-rev-rend*

"I've known Brian and Amy for many years and have seen in them a beautiful portrait of a loving couple who love God, their family, and their church. I have also seen their genuine and deep-felt desire to help men and women plant churches around the world that will be life-giving, not life-draining. That is the purpose of this book. Brian and Amy planted West Ridge many years ago and have survived and thrived through scores of ups and downs, which they now share with the rest of us so that we too can thrive. I encourage you to read this book and know that God's plan for church planting—and more importantly, his plan for you—is a good plan that will always exceed your wildest dreams."

—JONATHAN FALWELL
Pastor, Thomas Road Baptist Church

"Brian and Amy share their lives and their story in this book about the very personal world of church planting. I've known the Bloyes for fifteen years and cannot think of anyone more qualified to encourage and equip today's church-planting couples. Church planters will benefit from practical advice on everything from marriage to dealing with growth and change. *It's Personal* is a must-read for those who want to see the reality of planting a church."

—JOHNNY HUNT
Pastor, First Baptist Church,
Woodstock, Georgia

"I've trained thousands of planters, and I wish they all had this book. It will encourage church-planting families to make wise choices and to thrive as a family—leading to more productive ministry."

—ED STETZER
President of LifeWay Research and
Author of *Planting Missional Churches*

EXPONENTIAL
series

IT'S ~~NOT~~ PERSONAL

SURVIVING AND THRIVING ON THE JOURNEY OF CHURCH PLANTING

BRIAN & AMY BLOYE

FOREWORD BY ANDY STANLEY

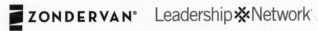

ZONDERVAN®   Leadership✳Network

ZONDERVAN.com/
AUTHORTRACKER
follow your favorite authors

We want to hear from you. Please send your comments about this book to us in care of zreview@zondervan.com. Thank you.

ZONDERVAN

It's Personal
Copyright © 2012 by Brian and Amy Bloye

This title is also available as a Zondervan ebook. Visit www.zondervan.com/ebooks.

Requests for information should be addressed to:
Zondervan, *Grand Rapids, Michigan* 49530

Library of Congress Cataloging-in-Publication Data

Bloye, Brian, 1965–
    It's personal : surviving and thriving on the journey of church planting / Brian and Amy Bloye.
      p. cm.
    ISBN 978-0-310-49454-6 (softcover)
   1. Church development, New. 2. Bloye, Brian, 1965– 3. Bloye, Amy, 1968– 4. West Ridge Church (Paulding County, Ga.)—History. I. Bloye, Amy, 1968– II. Title.
BV652.24.B58   2012
253'.2—dc23   2012001430

Cover design: Micah Kandros
Cover photography: iofoto / Veer
Interior design: Beth Shagene

Printed in the United States of America

---

12 13 14 15 16 17 18 /DCI/ 21 20 19 18 17 16 15 14 13 12 11 10 9 8 7 6 5 4 3 2 1

To our sons, Taylor and Zachary,
thank you for your passion, faithfulness, and support while we wrote this book. Thank you for loving God, the church, and lost and hurting people through all of your experiences as pastors' kids. You are warriors, and because of Jesus, you've got what it takes. We cannot wait to see the amazing things God is going to continue to do in your lives!

To our parents, John and Judy Bloye and Max and Nancy Mills.
You are our heroes. You have influenced our lives in such a huge way through your faithfulness and perseverance in marriage and ministry that we are blessed and compelled to pour out what has been given to us through your examples. Heaven seems closer and relationships are sweeter because of the huge impact you continue to have on our lives!

CONTENTS

FOREWORD

So you want to plant a church? Great! Just know this: it's not for the timid.

I have incredible respect for church planters. They're lovers of adventure, of getting to the front lines where the bullets are flying and where battles will be won or lost. Planting a successful church is one of the most demanding undertakings. It can also be one of the most satisfying. My friends Brian and Amy Bloye are about to give you a crash course in all that. These are dispatches from the front lines.

People say North Point was a church plant, and in some ways that's true. But we had a bank of a thousand people to start with. The Bloyes made it happen the hard way—maybe the way you're trying to make it happen. They loaded up a U-Haul, drove a few hundred miles away from everything familiar, and built from the ground up.

I've known Brian Bloye for more than ten years, and I've seen how it worked out at West Ridge Church. I found him to be both leader and learner, someone strong enough to point the way, but wise enough to make course corrections. As he and I talked, I felt the intensity of his commitment—not just to his church, but also to his family and his spiritual health. I saw that he grasped one of the church-planting essentials: most communities don't need another church, they need a *different kind* of church. Brian knew the truth in that. He insisted on it, sometimes at a high cost. One of the many lessons you will pull from this book is that church

planting demands all that you are and some of what you're not
—*yet.*

There are other books on this subject, but none that are more
practical, honest, or *raw* than this one. There might be a few pages
where you gulp and mutter, "Do I *really* want to do this?" Good—
it's a fair question. Just keep reading. Keep thinking. Keep praying. Because there will also be pages that inspire you, pages that
make you say, "I *really* want to do this." Then when you move on
to the front lines, you will be just a little better armed, a little more
battle wise.

—ANDY STANLEY

PREFACE

Do you remember *Seinfeld*'s "Soup Nazi" episode? As the character Kramer says, "He suffers for his soup." We get the point. Anything that is of great value will cost us something. Planting a church is just one example. (We can now add another: writing a book.) When Exponential Network and Leadership Network approached us about this project, we humbly accepted. We wanted to discuss issues that we see being lived out by so many church planters we encounter. Time after time, we've observed that there are *big* issues — but issues no one wants to bring up.

So yes, we felt called to write this book. But the process hasn't been easy. We've started each new chapter only to find that its themes were playing out in our everyday life. It's been true for us and even for our boys. These subjects have hit a little too close to home at times, but that's okay. We understand that nothing eternally significant happens without a certain amount of sacrifice.

As you read these pages, you may find that you disagree with a point or two. Church planting has its controversies and gray areas. We can only share what we've come to believe through our own journey, in the hope that others may find a nugget here and there to make their own experiences healthier and more effective. However, we'll promise you this: we'll be unflinchingly honest about the path we've traveled.

Now we invite you to share in the journey as we walk it again, with its high points and also its dark valleys. Church planting is difficult, unpredictable, and exhausting. But through it all, we've never ceased to believe that Jesus Christ and his church remain the one hope for this struggling world. That's why the sacrifice is worthwhile, and it's also why we're excited about this new, massive movement of church planting. God is doing an amazing thing.

We've seen it from the front lines — and we're honored to have this opportunity to share it with you.

CHAPTER 1

WHY IS CHURCH PLANTING SO PERSONAL?

We Are What We Build
(and Build What We Are)

I'm tagging along with Amy at the grocery store. It's my day off. We're walking through the produce section and chatting about what makes a great salad. The produce section is my favorite part of the store; I'm a fruit-oholic.

I push the cart around the first aisle, and now we're in the canned foods section — soup, beans, pineapple chunks. Amy loves it when I shop with her, because I always throw extra things in the cart! I'm a little impatient as I lean on the handle. We're in a hurry to get to the theater. We rarely miss our Friday afternoon movie date. The PA system plays a song I like. I hum along and do some people watching — and see a face I know in the coffee aisle. We'll call him Bill.

Bill has one of those handheld baskets on his arm. I see that *What are you doing here?* look on his face. For some reason, people are usually surprised to encounter their pastor at the grocery store. I clap a hand on Bill's shoulder. "How you been, man?"

He hesitates for just a moment. "Good. I'm good. You?"

What's up with Bill? He seems a little uncomfortable. My mind sorts through the Bill files and tells me I haven't seen his family at church for a while. So maybe that's it: *absentee guilt.* I need to subtly let him know that I'm not here to play the attendance card, so I'm extra friendly. "I hear your boy's going out for football. You must be excited."

"Oh ... Yeah, that's right. He is," says Bill. He looks down at the Colombian Blend in his hand for a moment, then says, "Brian, I've been meaning to tell you; we've been going to another church." He looks as if he's afraid I'm going to grab him by the throat and start choking him.

"Okay, well, that's great," I say, with a smile to let him know that it's all good. "Which church?" He tells me. "Lots of good things going on there," I say. "Their pastor is a friend of mine."

"Yeah," says Bill, relaxing a bit, a burden sliding from his shoulders. Still, it feels as if the two of us are in a funeral home, standing before the casket. I just hang loose for a minute, because if I walk away now, it will seem abrupt — as if I have no interest in someone who is no longer part of my church. Bill says, "It's just, you know, it's just more ... um, *right* for my family where we are now."

"Tell me a little more about that," I say. "I'm interested."

"Well," Bill says slowly, "I don't know, I guess we feel we're getting *fed* more where we are now. Nothing personal, Brian! It's just a better fit, especially since our kids are getting older. You know we love you and Amy — and we are going to continue to send all of our unchurched friends to West Ridge."

"Absolutely, Bill, you just be sure you plug in wherever you are. That's the big thing, to find the best place for you to serve God; and whenever there's anything we can do for you, you know where to find us."

"I appreciate that, Brian. I really do. You say hi to Amy for me."

"I'll do that," I say with a smile, and I go to catch up with my wife.

She's in the pasta section. "Vermicelli or angel hair?" she asks without looking up.

"Angel hair."

"Was that Bill?"

"Yeah, that was him. We caught up. I'll tell you about it in the truck."

We spot a couple other members of our church before we check out. We smile, chat a few minutes, and promise to pray for some of the needs they mention. Finally we've loaded all our groceries into the backseat, and we're in the truck and buckled up.

"Okay, tell me about Bill," says Amy.

"He and his family have changed churches."

"Oh. They weren't angry or unhappy or anything, were they?"

"Not really—at least I don't think so. They just feel their new church is a better fit."

"I see."

We sit quietly for a moment. Amy says with a grin, "Let me guess. He said they love West Ridge and it's not personal, right?"

"Pretty much."

"So why do we feel it personally whenever someone leaves, whenever they say they fit better somewhere else?"

"Because, in a certain way, it is absolutely personal. No matter how much we're committed to God's kingdom, we're just going to feel it this way, because building a church is a personal thing." I turn the key, crank the engine, and look over my shoulder before starting to pull out of our parking space.

"You can say that again," Amy says. "It's like giving birth. The church is a part of who we are, and we feel very protective of it."

"And it's about love and people," I add. "The little bits of ourselves that we pour into building a church that is actually a family."

Amy nods. "Makes me think about our boys. Either of us would give our lives for Taylor and Zach, but think about this: What if one of my friends came up to me and said, 'I just love Taylor. You must be very proud of him. Zach, not so much—nothing personal. But I love Taylor!'"

"I would *not* like to hear that."

"Because our two boys are the world to us. Both of them. We've poured our lives into Taylor and Zachary. So if you tell us you don't like one of our boys, well, that's pretty personal."

"I think you've hit it," I reply. "Those of us in the ministry don't punch the clock and go home and draw a curtain over that part of life. What I speak about during my sermons is so much of what Christ has done inside of me and what I've learned from studying his Word."

"You can only speak as God leads you, and you know that you can't please all the people all the time."

"Yeah. In ministry, you'd go crazy if you didn't get that through your thick skull. Still, I can tell you that I've prayed for Bill. I've prayed for his family, and when I stand up to bring a message from God, I'm wanting, from the deepest part of my soul, for him to use me to help Bill and guys like him connect with God. When I meet with the staff at the church to help plan the worship service, everything we do is geared for that. The message, the songs, the videos — these are not *products*. We've poured ourselves all over those things."

We fall silent as we continue the drive home. Amy looks out at the houses and parks, the joggers and the kids playing. I know she is thinking about the personal price of ministry in the real world. It can consume you if you're not very careful, very discerning. It's the art of painting precise boundary lines.

This is a truth for any pastor's family, but church planting takes it to the next level. It's one of the ultimate challenges in church leadership. Building a new church forces you to cling to God, to become totally dependent upon him. The best and worst moments in your life are going to come. You're going to celebrate on the mountain peak one day, grieve in the valley the next.

We're thinking about all these things, Amy and I.

"If we had to do this all over again, would you do it the same way?" asks Amy.

"Yeah, I think I would. But you can't really separate the church part. Our journey. Ministry. Marriage. Family. They all seem scrambled up into one thing."

"Exactly. Have we done the best we could to keep them untangled?"

I think for a moment. "I believe so. I'm not saying we've nailed it. I can think of a few little do-overs I wouldn't mind. But you know what? I can't imagine missing out on all that God has done here."

"Good," Amy says with a big smile. "I agree! I just wanted to hear you say it."

"It's been personal," I say. "It's gotten *very* personal at times. When I stand back on a Sunday morning and take a look at our church—you know, wide-angle lens, the big picture—I see something that has God's fingerprints all over it, but also mine. And yours. And the friends and family who have been with us from the very beginning. I guess a painter can create a picture of some beautiful landscape, and it's a picture of something nobody but God could make—but art lovers can look at that picture and know exactly who the painter was. Because it's *personal*. It has the painter's *style*. A church is built from the blood, sweat, and tears of the people who build it in God's power."

Amy is thinking about this book we've agreed to write. "So how do we explain this to church planters?"

"Now, there's a good question," I say, just as we pull into our driveway. "I guess I would start by saying what we've just said —that it's very personal. That it's the adventure of a lifetime. You can expect to pay a high price, and if you hang in there, you will have the opportunity to see God do amazing things that only he can do. Because it's personal to him. He personally gave his own Son for each person we are trying to reach."

"Yeah, that's good."

"Then I'd look a church planter in the eye and ask him to tell me about his calling."

"Good point."

As we bring in our groceries, our minds go back to the beginning of our story.

In the Beginning

When does life begin for a congregation?

A church is like a child. It is a living being long before it sees the light of day. As far as our community was concerned, West Ridge Church was born on September 7, 1997. But it was conceived months earlier, in March of 1996, in the hearts of Amy and me. We had felt a call to start a church, and there was a moment in our time together when we knew we were saying yes to that call. From that moment, it was like planning for a birth. We had questions, dreams, hope, fear, excitement, good advice, and naive ideas. Just as expectant parents begin to change once they start the nine-month countdown, so we were changed by knowing that God wanted to use us to bring a brand-new church — a fresh new part of the body of Christ — into life and service.

Accepting the call to serve an existing church, of course, is a thrill. You get to know the church, with its people, its distinct personality, and its special traditions. We would instinctively adapt ourselves in certain ways to fit into the culture of that congregation. Planting a church is different. As uncomfortable as this description might feel, there is a sense in which a church plant is a reflection of your personal relationship with Christ. Yes, God does the true spiritual planting, the watering, and the nurture, and only he can bring the harvest. But people who have helped plant churches know what I mean: There's no need to adapt ourselves to an existing church culture. We will create one from scratch. We'll launch the traditions, according to our understanding of how church should be. This lets us emphasize the practices we've found most helpful and avoid the ones we think are outdated or just wrong. The new church will look like our *personal* under-standing of what a church should be. Therefore it's personal.

Amy and I each came from families who planted churches. We understood that accepting the call was no small decision; it would utterly change everything about our lives — including where we live, because of the imperative of moving to a new part of the country. But it was very clear to both of us that this was what God wanted us to do. The vision was *powerful*. We shared it without question or hesitation. We were going to move to the Atlanta met-ropolitan area, and there would be no looking back, no compromise. This ship was going to sail, or we would sink with it.

Today we lead seminars for church planters, and we look out at the eager faces, the eyes filled with the intoxication of something new and thrilling. We love to see that look, knowing that the Holy Spirit has placed it there. Even so, we don't sugarcoat what lies ahead for these servants of God. Amy and I make it clear that the two most difficult tasks we've ever encountered — individually or as a couple — are:

1. Raising children

2. Raising a church

We tell them to know, going in, that their marriage is as strong as it can possibly be, because that marriage will be tested from every angle, every weak spot. We tell them that planting a church will challenge everything they think they know about raising a family. We tell them that it will unmask every flaw in their leader-ship style and every blemish in their personal character, and that they will be introduced to levels of spiritual warfare they never knew existed. I doubt we can find any plainer way to make the statement that this is a *personal* quest. Your experience in planting a church will go the way of your personal relationship with Jesus Christ. Your absolute devotion to him will be reflected in how you build the church; your blind spots in following him will play out as flaws in what you build.

In the end, should all go well, you will stand with some satisfaction and see a church that is the power of Christ living and working in this world. It will also bear your DNA in every brick, every carpet fiber, every program, every quirk, so that when someone comes up to you and begins expressing opinions about the weaknesses of your church (even though you shouldn't feel this way), you will hear all of it as though someone were questioning your personal relationship with Christ.

Yet for Amy and me, even when those words are hurtful, even when someone brings pain to a member of our family, even when we feel weary and envious of our friends with simpler jobs, *saner* jobs, jobs they can leave at the office—the words of Bill Hybels wander into our minds: "The church," he said, "is the hope of the world." And again we feel deeply stirred. Yes, the church is truly the hope of the world. Even with its warts, its demands, and its irregular people, the church is the hands of Christ, still touching and healing; the feet of Christ, still walking the paths of human

---

Having been in church planting for a while, we can say it's impossible *not* to take personally many of the aspects of our ministry. We have grieved as next-door neighbors, longtime church members, and even close friends have chosen to leave our church, whether the decision was positive or not. If we have loved people, it will always be personal. However, after we have grieved, we've learned to die to ourselves. We're not in this for our personal comfort and relationships. We're in this for His glory! That enables us to have courageous conversations, make tough calls, stay the course, and lead for an audience of one!

— Shawn and Tricia Lovejoy,
Mountainlake Church, Cumming, GA

need; the words of Christ, still speaking the one and only truth to a world caught up in deadly confusion.

We feel it's worth the price we pay.

Why It's Worth It

It just takes the right word, whispered by a still, small voice in our ears, and we know it's time to go back to work. We need a reminder of the call we first accepted a decade and a half ago. It helps to remember that Jesus gave his precious, perfect life for the church—not just the theoretical church but each and every place in this world where two or more gather in his name. Jesus looked upon the hate-filled faces of the men who drove the spikes through his hands and feet, and he forgave them. He prayed that those soldiers would find his love in the arms of the church he was dying to build. He endured all the pain this world had to give him, because he could see beyond the rocky terrain of Calvary. He could see the church. It may be flawed and frustrating, but it is still God's way of showing his grace and power to this world.

The church is God's light in the vast darkness around us. Jesus, better than anyone who ever lived, knew people and their flaws. But he kept his eyes on what the church could be, and he exchanged his life for that vision. That's what Amy and I feel called to do.

There is a particularly moving passage in Hebrews 11 about what it means to be a leader who walks by the courage of genuine faith. The chapter sets out a roll call of the great heroes of the Old Testament—Abraham, Jacob, Joseph, and the rest. These were people who followed God with simple belief. The passage concludes:

All these people were still living by faith when they died. They did not receive the things promised; they only saw them and welcomed them from a distance, admitting that they were foreigners and strangers on earth. People who say such things show that they are looking for a country of their own. If they had been thinking of the country they had left, they would have had opportunity to return. Instead, they were longing for a better country — a heavenly one. Therefore God is not ashamed to be called their God, for he has prepared a city for them.

—HEBREWS 11:13–16

All those Bible heroes were people who never looked back. Their lives were not easy — just victorious, from God's perspective. This is the course set out for us as leaders and as planters. The great rewards we discuss are often ahead and never visible. But we keep patting the soil, depending on the rain and the seasons. We are planters. We plant the gospel in cities devastated by sin, because we truly believe there is another country, the heavenly country described in Hebrews. It is our heart to keep loving these people, teaching them, and shepherding them as they grow to be fully devoted followers of Jesus Christ.

It happens too. Though we talk about the tough days and the trials, God often shows up in the midst of our struggles — *especially* shows up in those struggles. He moves in people, he changes hearts, he fixes what is broken, and he performs miracles that leave no doubt that he is real and present. We've seen God do things that have been far beyond what we've ever imagined. If it all ended right now, we'd say it's all been worthwhile.

It's Been a Ride!

Amy and I experienced moments of doubt, particularly in the early days of building West Ridge. There were times when we wondered how in the world we could go on, where in the world the funds to pay our staff and our bills would come from. Perhaps we thought back about the comfort and security of the wonderful church we had left, hundreds of miles away. But we understood the meaning of those words from Hebrews: "If they had been thinking of the country they had left, they would have had opportunity to return."

Sure, there was always that opportunity. But we never really came close to running up the flag of surrender, because we were serious about our calling. We had so much to learn, but we did have a basic understanding of how God works. We knew that we were being toned, sculpted, and conditioned for something eternally significant, and that if we could only have the strength to walk by faith, the fruit would come, and come in abundance. Today we are making disciples. We are baptizing new believers, sending out missionaries, reshaping our community in the name of Christ. We've given our blood, our sweat, and our tears, but we've learned that those can be very strong fertilizer in planting.

If we could do it all again, we might tweak a few things along the way, but we would sign up again without a second thought. So yes, it's worth it. But that doesn't mean you want to stumble into this task blindfolded. The Boy Scouts are onto something — we need to be prepared. You'll need preparation physically, mentally, emotionally, and spiritually.

No easy formula will ensure success for your church plant. No Bible college or seminary can ensure that your task will be easy and comfy. Neither will this book provide any shortcuts from some of the rougher roads you'll find yourself walking. You can read a library of books about climbing Mount Everest, but nothing will quite prepare you for the real-world experience of going out there, up there, and taking it on. Climbing is the real education.

Church planting is the ultimate mountain ascent. It's a quest that forces you to watch your footing, to cling to God, and to be certain that you're tightly roped to your fellow climbers. You'll be breathless at times, exhausted at times, but we'll promise you this: the view is indescribable. At the summit, you'll begin to see the world as God sees it. Church planting is an adventure. It's a God-ward climb.

And yes, you will take it very personally.

> The advance of gospel proclamation is most likely found in church planting. Church planting has become the preferred evangelistic strategy in North America and around the world. As God is redeeming people and gathering them together in churches, they become new outposts for kingdom work. New churches intentionally focus outward, as they are forced to reach people in their communities and think outside the box.
>
> — Ed and Donna Stetzer,
> Grace Church, Nashville, TN

CHAPTER 2

HOW DO YOU KNOW YOU ARE CALLED TO PLANT A CHURCH?

Not Every "Cool" Thing Is a God Thing

It was two o'clock in the morning in Virginia, and we were sitting up way too late again. Just shooting the breeze. It was November of 1995. "I can't put my finger on it," I was saying to Amy. "I just don't have that feeling that I'm exactly where God wants me to be."

Amy sighed. "Honey," she said, "you're ministering to hundreds of students at Thomas Road. You're getting some wonderful speaking opportunities outside the church." She and I both knew I was discontented.

"True. And I'm training Liberty students who will be pastors all over the world. I'm teaching a seminary class on student ministry. On top of all that, we just bought a new house."

Amy held up five fingers and started counting our blessings on them. "You have a great student ministry, you get to teach, you get to speak, you get to travel, and the church gives you almost complete freedom — you can choose to do ministry anywhere and everywhere as you feel led. Most student pastors out there would *kill* for your position."

"We wouldn't want anyone to do that," I joked.

"You get my point. It's a dream job. So how is it that you don't feel you're in the place where God wants you to be?"

"I feel some kind of discontent," I said with a shrug. "Even discouragement at times, in the middle of experiences that should be satisfying."

Amy sat in the bed with her arms wrapped around her knees, thinking. "Brian, what if you could do anything right now, have any job? The sky's the limit—dream big. What comes to mind?"

I sat quietly for a moment, then said, "Amy, what would you say if I suggested we pack up, get out of here, and go start a church somewhere?"

Here's the strange part: I had not particularly been considering this idea. Becoming a church planter was not on my radar. But when my wife asked me the question in the middle of a November night, that's what came out.

Amy said, "You mean, with no people? No money? No building? Nothing?"

I said, "Exactly! Doesn't that sound exciting to you?"

I waited for the confirmation that we were both feeling the call. Amy said, "No! Just the thought of that turns my stomach!"

I laughed. "Okay, sure, it sounds scary."

"Yes, it does. But you know what, Brian? If that's what God wants, I would be ready to go for it."

I smiled as I recognized one more reason why I loved my wife so much. *She got it.* She understood about following Christ wherever he leads. But why would the idea of church planting turn her stomach?

I knew the answer. Both of us had a small history with church start-ups. We came from families that had been involved in them. My parents planted two different churches, the first in Boynton Beach, Florida, in 1983. I graduated from high school, moved with my parents to Florida to help with the initial work, and made plans to attend college in South Florida.

It wasn't a good experience, to say the least. After six months I moved back to Texas, and after a year my parents shut down the church and followed me. In 1985 they tried again in Howell,

Michigan, and that church is still active. So ten years later, at a ministerial crossroads, I had seen two very different models of the church-planting experience.

Amy's parents planted a church in Salisbury, North Carolina. That experience was somewhere between the two I'd seen — the church survived by merging with another congregation. What we learned from all three plants was that it's very difficult to start a new church. That may seem hard to believe as you drive across the countryside and see churches on nearly every street corner. It looks easy, it sounds easy. It's not. Church planting is financial warfare. It is an emotional, spiritual obstacle course, and an extreme test for the family.

When my husband first told me he felt God was calling him to start a church, I was scared to death, but I was careful to listen and not to overreact (at least until he left the room). I knew God was doing something special in my husband's life, so I decided to remain open to the possibilities. As I prayed and watched his walk and faith increasing, it became 100 percent clear to me that this was God and we had to move forward together.

— Danielle Newsome

It sounds really simple, but I know God called me to start a church because the "call" in my life was as clear as anything God had ever spoken to me about. It was literally a "burning bush" experience, where God directly told me to start a church. As I pursued that call, huge confirmations in our steps of faith and answered prayers led to even more clarity and resolve that this truly was God's path for us.

— Christian Newsome,
Journey Church International,
Lee Summit, MO

Feeding the Fire

I understood that just because Amy and I didn't share the same vision, it didn't mean God wasn't speaking to us. He wanted us to wrestle with the idea a little bit. We didn't need to make any decisions with cheap and easy bravado. We needed to wrestle with God, the way Jacob did. What we did share was this: a strong perception that God was stoking a fire inside us, building up our spiritual energy to be part of something amazing that only he could do. We had talked about this, and we knew that a great part of faith is being involved in endeavors that are so startling that people could never grab the credit. That's the formula for glorifying God.

We both knew we had a fruitful ministry and a comfortable existence right where we were. We had a good marriage, a new house, our first child, and soul-satisfying work. The life of the true disciple isn't about comfort, however. It's about walking in faith, taking risks, attempting great things for God and expecting great things from him. At times it also includes suffering and failure. So we both understood that comfort and security weren't at the top of our list. It was simply a matter of pursuing God's heart until we found out what he wanted us to do.

Two months passed. In January of 1996 I made plans to meet my dad at a Promise Keepers conference at the Georgia Dome in Atlanta. Promise Keepers was in its heyday at that time. I looked forward to being part of the gathering, but I especially welcomed the rare opportunity to spend time with my dad. I remember that week so well — the dynamics of forty-two thousand pastors coming together to praise God and commit themselves to becoming better spiritual leaders in their marriages and families. Chuck Swindoll stepped to the podium and led us in a study of Isaiah 6. I sat forward to hear what he would say, and soon I had the feeling that he was speaking directly to me.

Who Will Go for Us?

Dr. Swindoll brought the story to life — a story from ancient Judah.

King Uzziah was on his deathbed, wasted away from leprosy. His attendants kept him in seclusion as an era ended. No one knew what was in store for the proud nation. The prophets understood that it had been a time of physical prosperity and spiritual emptiness. We've seen this happen: when people grow fat and comfortable, they lose their spiritual edge. They forget the way to God's presence. God wanted the people to see that just as their king, once so healthy, withered away, the nation would do the same.

Meanwhile God brought an incredible vision to a young man named Isaiah. It was a hard and uncomfortable message, because enemies were at the gate. We don't know where Isaiah was, or what he was doing, when the vision came. But it shook him to his soul and changed him forever. Suddenly Isaiah found himself standing in the throne room of the Almighty. At a great height, in awesome glory, the Lord sat enthroned. The air was filled with six-winged seraphim, angels of fire. They were calling out, "Holy, holy, holy is the LORD Almighty; the whole earth is full of his glory" (Isa. 6:3). Isaiah's senses were overpowered by all that was happening. He knew he couldn't look upon the face of the Lord; he was too human, too unworthy in his humanity. He cried out, "Woe to me! . . . I am ruined!" (v. 5).

Have you ever had a moment when your whole life was put in its proper perspective? Isaiah could see the glory of God and the reality of his own sinfulness. He understood just how deep a gap there was between heaven and earth. How could there be any hope for his family, his friends, his nation?

Then one of the angels came to him. It had to be terrifying! But the angel opened his hand and produced a chunk of burning coal.

He pushed it toward Isaiah's mouth. Can you imagine heating charcoal on your grill, then sticking a piece into your mouth? Yet Isaiah felt grace, not judgment. He felt God's love and power. The angel said that Isaiah's guilt had been removed; his sins had been taken care of. Then God spoke, and this is what he said: "Whom shall I send? And who will go for us?" Isaiah immediately cried out, "Here am I. Send me!" (v. 8).

Isaiah had received his calling. I imagine he had no doubts about it after that experience; don't you agree?

The Word That Broke Me

As Dr. Swindoll took us through the narrative, I stood in Isaiah's sandals. I knew what it was like to say, "Woe is me!" and to know my unworthiness, just as the young prophet did. I felt a powerful sense of God's holiness. Jack Hayford, the great pastor and worship leader, came to the podium and led us in the majestic hymn taken from Isaiah 6 and Revelation 4, "Holy, Holy, Holy." Hearing forty-two thousand pastors sing that particular chorus was moving, to say the least. I wasn't at the foot of God's throne, as Isaiah had been — but I felt about as close to it as ever before in my life. All we needed was a few angels and a few charcoal grills.

I stood and looked at the ecstatic, joyful faces around me — people worshiping, people experiencing the goodness and power of God. I was feeling it too, but I was wrestling as the prophet had. Everyone else was standing to sing. I was sitting, feeling a great weight on my shoulders. Finally I came to the end of myself. I stood and lifted my hands. My tears began to flow. I prayed, "God, I don't know where all of this is leading, but I will do whatever you want me to do. I'm available."

I realized that I might have to give up a lot of things. I had a fruitful ministry, but I had also gotten comfortable, and comfort can become one more idol. I realized I was making a life-changing decision. I felt so much like Isaiah, sensing his unworthiness before a holy God. I had come to the end of myself, which is always the beginning of God revealing to us what he wants us to see—which always involves bringing him glory. I whispered, "Here I am, Lord; send me." I added no fine print or disclaimers, no maps specifying where I would or would not consent to go. I made a great blank check of my life and signed it over to God. *Any way you want to spend it, Lord.*

There in the Georgia Dome, I was overcome by what the Spirit of God was doing within me. I made my way to the aisle and then down to the center of the arena. At the front of the stage, several pastors were lying on the floor in prayer and surrender, and I joined them. I pressed my nose to the floor and let the tears flow. What I felt was brokenness, and God placed a verse on my heart: "Joshua told the people, 'Consecrate yourselves, for tomorrow the LORD will do amazing things among you'" (Josh. 3:5).

When it came time to return to my seat, I felt as if I could have caught a breeze and floated up to the upper deck. I was that much lighter. The wrestling was over, pride had gone down to defeat, and God had won. At the same time, something had opened up within me; I felt I had plowed through some of the obstructions that had kept me from hearing what God wanted me to do. To this day, I think back to that moment as one of the true spiritual highlights of my life. Now all I had to do was explain it all to Amy. I felt that God was seeing if I was willing to lay everything down and say yes to him, before he would bring our hearts together as a couple.

Are You Willing to Follow?

Brian had a lot to tell me; I (Amy) could see that clearly enough. Something had changed inside him, and I was as eager to hear about it as he was to tell about it. He sat beside me and painted a picture in words, describing the setting of the Georgia Dome, the crowd of men dedicating themselves to God, and especially what the Holy Spirit had shown him about himself. Brian called it his "Isaiah 6 moment."

Before this day, I would have definitely told you my husband was fully dedicated to God. But I could see that he had taken his commitment to the next level. He worried because I hadn't been there, because it wasn't *my* Isaiah 6 moment. But as I listened, I was buying in completely. I believe that women want to follow a man who is passionately following God.

That's how it felt to me. As Brian unpacked his insights, I understood what he meant about being too comfortable, and I knew it was true for me too. God wasn't just calling my husband; he was calling us as a couple. Brian said, "Amy, I think God is moving us out of Lynchburg."

There was firm conviction in his voice. I know he wondered how I was going to respond. I offered four words: "Where are we going?"

"I have no idea," he replied. Then a big smile came across his face, and he said, "But it's going to be fun!" And he gave me a big hug, thanking me for believing in him. After all, we were in a new house with boxes yet to be unpacked, and we had no real plan. At this point, we weren't set on planting a church, just on being obedient. I think God was simply asking, "Are you willing to follow, without knowing where?" And our answer was yes.

So even with so much up in the air, I was standing with my husband on this decision. It was really all about believing in Brian and seeing the change in him. But my own God moment in the process was yet to come. It happened on the day we went to meet with Dr. Falwell.

Preparing for Liftoff

I (Brian) was thankful for Amy. I was asking a lot, and she responded with dedication and enthusiasm. After all, we were a team. This was a journey we were taking together. During the next few months we put out feelers. Only two things were clear: we were supposed to leave Lynchburg, and we were supposed to leave student ministry. With this much to go on, we networked with churches and leaders over the phone and in person. This was the only way we knew to explore what God had planned for us.

Call after call, visit after visit, we ran into dead ends. We would talk for ten minutes, and there would be the strong conviction that this wasn't God's will for us. There would be nothing to do but politely close the conversation and move on. Soon — the end of March 1996, to be precise — Amy and I realized it was time to bring our pastor, Dr. Jerry Falwell, into the loop. In those days, when people asked me the name of my boss, I knew I'd either have to pucker or duck. No one seemed to have neutral feelings about Jerry Falwell.

Amy and I certainly weren't neutral: we loved him and we loved his family. We were graduates of Liberty University, the college he founded. We spent any number of evenings as guests in his home. Dr. Falwell performed our wedding ceremony and dedicated our older son, Taylor. We felt his generous affection in ministry and as a couple. Dr. Falwell passed away several years ago, and we still miss him. But in 1996 he was my mentor, and we knew we needed his counsel on the call we had received.

Sitting in his office and waiting to speak, we couldn't have been more nervous. It's not that we didn't expect to receive his blessing — just that we knew God was leading us somewhere else, and we hoped that Dr. Falwell's love for us wouldn't create the temptation to please an earthly father figure rather than a heavenly Father.

"Doc," I began, "we have sought God's will and prayed for a

long time on what direction to take in ministry. I felt God's Spirit tugging at my heart, urging me to follow wherever he might lead. We've been so happy here that we have a million reasons to stay. But when God calls ... well, you know. We hope you won't try to convince us to stay, because we have a powerful sense of leading in this thing, even though we don't have a clue where we're going."

Dr. Falwell always filled a room. He was great in stature, of course, but he had a charisma that was just as large. He had a personal presence that people found unforgettable. He leaned back in his chair and listened to my impassioned statement, then laughed. He couldn't have been more gracious. Of *course* the Lord had great things in store for us. Of *course* we would be led to some other place of need at the right time. He said, "You guys need to go and start a new church."

"Really?" I asked. "Just like that?"

"Sure! Pick a major city, one that's growing quickly. Move there and build your church from the ground up."

Dr. Falwell had mentored quite a few young ministers. He could see that God was at work. He came around the desk and shook my hand, gave Amy a hug, and let us know that he was grateful for the time together God had given us. We thanked him and told him we would pray over his advice. He promised that as long as he was around, we could count on his prayer support.

We knew we were called to plant a church when we could think, talk, and dream about nothing else. In our case, God called us to plant a church before he called us to a specific city. We had a vision to simply reach people who were far from God and make a difference in our city. God gave us a big vision that came to life with small steps of obedience.

— Steven and Holly Furtick,
Elevation Church, Charlotte, NC

I didn't know until we walked out of his office what Amy thought about all this. I saw immediately that there was a skip in her step and a grin on her face. I remembered her saying that the thought of a church plant all but made her sick. Now I was the one with a knot in my stomach. I asked, "What do you think about what Doc said?"

"Church planting!" she said. "Doesn't that sound exciting?"

God's direction for us couldn't have been more clear.

The Blackaby Effect

As the path began to take shape, God was at work filling out the depth of our calling. He put people, ideas, and even books in our path to help us understand how and why we were following him. As an example, we had been reading *Experiencing God* by Dr. Henry Blackaby. This was what sparked our realization that God was stirring up something inside us that we couldn't define. The book has helped transform the spiritual lives of many people, and we were no exceptions.

Dr. Blackaby offers a powerful insight on divine guidance. He says that if you want to know God's will, the last thing you should do is create a plan and invite God to go along with you on it. That puts things precisely backward. Instead, he says, find out where God is already at work and join him there. Look for a lit fire, then bring kindling.

We spent a lot of time reflecting on that idea, realizing that most of us live our faith inside out, upside down, and backward most of the time. We figure God is our copilot, as the bumper sticker says. We decide where we would like to go, then offer a nice prayer over it as we make our plans. It's an odd approach to the sovereign ruler of the universe.

What did this realization mean for our future? If Amy and I did demographic studies, compared different cities, and so forth, what if we were only inviting God along on our own plans? How would we know when we found the place where *he* was at work and wanted *our* involvement? We puzzled over Psalm 37:4, which reads, "Delight yourself also in the LORD, and He shall give you the desires of your heart" (NKJV). Did that verse mean that if we sought God, he would give us what we wanted? That sounded like a copilot faith. Maybe instead it meant that the more we chased after the Lord, the more we would be infected by his desires, and what he wanted would become what *we* wanted. That sounded much better.

God does give us the desires of our heart when we seek him; the point is that he places his desires in our heart and then he fulfills them. The more we pursue his heart, the more we reflect who he is. Spiritual maturity is seeing what God sees and wanting what he wants. The two of us decided that the most important thing we could do was to leave the details to God and simply focus on drawing closer to him. Then it would be a matter of waiting for the Blackaby effect, opening our eyes to suddenly see the place where God was at work and stepping up to enlist for service.

In 1996 we traveled to Atlanta for a birthday and to help celebrate a wedding. During my sister-in-law's birthday dinner, one subject kept coming up: Paulding County and its explosive growth. Our friends and relatives couldn't contain their excitement about watching their little corner of the world become a major population center. As we listened to all the talk, we found ourselves charmed by the town and the county we were hearing about. We didn't know it immediately, but the Blackaby effect was setting in. At some point we looked at one another, and each knew what the other was thinking. Here was the place where God was at work and was calling for helpers. It was as if we heard the voice of Jesus saying, "I tell you, open your eyes and look at the fields! They are ripe for harvest" (John 4:35).

Paulding County, just northwest of Atlanta, was ripe to say

the least—in April of 1996, the seventh-fastest-growing county in the United States. It was 93.7 percent unchurched, a figure that shocked us, since it was in the middle of the Bible Belt and there were churches on every corner. Its fields and forests were giving way to neighborhoods that were sprouting like the Southern kudzu. Shopping centers, roads, and restaurants were being laid down, and families—young families in particular—were arriving. Business commuters were putting down roots, babies were being born, and everywhere was the urgent need for Christ's touch and a true reflection of the gospel.

Up to this time, God had said no to all the directions for ministry we had investigated—except one. He had not warmed our hearts toward any particular place—except one. We felt he was leading us toward Paulding County, Georgia.

Confirmation

We all need those moments of true clarity, when God seems to nail down the map that's been coming together in our minds. In those moments, we feel led, but we really want to be sure.

We were visiting Georgia again when we met with the director of the local Baptist association. We didn't necessarily have strong denominational intentions at this point; honestly, we looked forward to the freedom that accompanies beginning a church plant. But it was important to get to know people in the area, to network, and to learn what we could. Bob Franklin directed the Noonday Baptist Association, and he heard about our intentions and invited us to his office. We immediately responded to his warmth and passion for churches. Behind his desk was a huge map of the area, dotted with little plastic pins of different colors. It was clear that he knew and cared for every hill and highway, while we were newcomers without much of a clue.

We chatted for a few moments, got to know each other, and

listened as Bob told us about the work of his association. Then he said, "Tell me again about the area where you feel God is calling you."

"Well, it's generally the place where Highways 92 and 278 cross in Paulding County," I replied. "I have family nearby, so it's the only area we're at all familiar with."

Bob smiled, rose from his chair, and moved his finger toward that place on the map. "Do you see the color of pin I've placed on that exact spot? It's red. Now, all these blue pins you see are existing churches. The red pin means we need one planted *exactly there*. I placed this pin here two years ago. Brian and Amy, we've been praying for two years for God to send someone to plant a church in that community."

We were speechless. He reached his arms across the desk and took our hands, and tears came into his eyes. "Church planting is kingdom work," he said.

There was a lump in my throat. When you know you are the answer to two years of dedicated prayer, you feel very humbled. You can't even begin to imagine questioning something that is happening by such clear divine appointment. Amy and I wanted to be involved in kingdom work. As we left that meeting, we didn't speak much but savored that incredible feeling that comes when God speaks right into everyday activity.

We went from there to another meeting, this one with a man named Mac Riggs, who was missions pastor with First Baptist Church of Woodstock, Georgia. I had met the senior pastor, Johnny Hunt, at a meeting. He'd said, "Let us come alongside you and support what you're doing." Without knowing us personally, he ended up giving us more financial support than anyone who knew us well. His church is one of the great ones, and we'll always be grateful.

Mac Riggs turned out to be a strong advocate for us in our early days. He had a realistic, pragmatic point of view and was willing to ask the hard questions. At this early meeting, he said, "Okay, so you've left everything that's comfortable to you. You've pulled up stakes and made the move, put everything on the line for this church. What if you fail?"

"Then we'll just go and do something else," I answered. "We'll flip burgers. Or we'll go apply for jobs at Walmart." He sat and looked at me, surprised that I could be just as raw and realistic as he could. "Look," I said, "God hasn't brought us down here to leave us high and dry. If our church plant fails, then we'll ask him what he wants us to do next. It's not going to mean he doesn't love us. We don't think that way. But I'll tell you this — we're ready to plant this church or die trying."

He nodded approval, and a slow smile came to his face. "You know," he said, "church planting is kingdom work." Amy and I started laughing. We had talked to two very different men, and each had boiled it down to the same term.

Kingdom work.

We felt confirmation. We knew God wanted us to start West Ridge Church in Paulding County, Georgia, north and west of Atlanta. Destiny had a zip code for us now, and that felt good. Just as we had hoped and prayed, we had seen the place where God was at work. It was time to plant for a harvest.

Questions to Think About

West Ridge was conceived in our hearts during a birthday dinner — a family gathering that we never expected would launch our future. We came to northwest Atlanta for reasons related to our family, and left with ideas about God's family. All we knew at the time was that this was something we were called to do. With our experience of church plants, neither of us had a burning desire to go somewhere and start a new congregation. But we felt an authentic call from God to leave our home, and then we felt specific guidance to plant a church in the northwest metro Atlanta area.

Fifteen years later, of course, church planting is quite the trend. It has become a full-fledged movement in American Christianity, so that pastors and leaders are jumping in with both feet. In recent decades, we've seen a seeker-sensitive movement, a purpose-driven movement, a house church movement, and now church planting is the latest thing. And there's nothing wrong with that. God uses changing methods in changing times. He'll do anything and everything to reach people.

As excited as we are about the planting movement, we do have some questions about what we are seeing. We've watched too many people rush into church planting for the wrong reasons, and it almost never ends well. Here are some questions we often pose to people who come to us for advice as church planters.

1. Are You Certain of Your Calling?

There is only one reason to plant a church (or do anything else, for that matter). That is the sturdy conviction that it's the one and only thing God wants you to do.

In business, young entrepreneurs read the *Wall Street Journal*, follow hot trends, and decide the timing is right to start this or that business. It's a perfectly sound career strategy, but the church is a divine institution that doesn't operate on human terms. I see many great marketing people and great entrepreneurs who aren't necessarily great long-term planters. They can gather a crowd, put together services and ministries, and do all these basics, but are they willing to take the people on a long-term spiritual journey?

We think of full-time ministry as a vocation, and it is. But it must also be a calling, and it must be carried out under the full guidance of God. We tell people, "If there's anything in the world you can do other than church planting, you should do that." That sounds severe, but we want people to understand that the task is going to be more difficult and demanding than they're likely to realize. Another way of saying this is, "Don't plant a church because you think you can do it. Plant one if you think you *must* do it."

It's the same with marriage: we shouldn't marry someone we think we can live with; we should marry someone we can't live *without*. You need to feel called, and your calling needs to feel confirmed.

2. Have You Considered Your Marriage and Family?

As Jesus said, a house divided cannot stand. For the challenge of planting a church, the home must be a rock. Amy and I totally agreed that we were doing what God wanted, not for one of us but for *both* of us. This is why it was so crucial that my wife should feel co-ownership of the vision God had given me. If she hadn't, that would have been one of several red flags that would have told me I needed to stop and reconsider.

That's true for any big step we take in life, not simply church planting. But the greater the challenge, the more critical the need for unity in marriage and family. The husband and wife will need each other more than ever, and in deeper ways. We'll devote a chapter to this subject later, but for now it's important to understand that the state of your marriage looms large in the question of your calling.

What about children? Planters need to realize that they'll be combining the two most difficult jobs of their lives: raising children and raising a church. It can be quite a juggling feat! There will be times when the two are at odds, other times when choices will have to be made. We will consider these questions a few pages ahead, but at the point of calling, the planter must look into the future and think, *Can I be a fully engaged, godly parent while taking on the adventure of building a new church?*

3. Do You Have a Support Network?

The irony is that the stronger our circle of support, the more difficult it is to leave it behind and follow God's trail. This was the problem we struggled with for months. We loved our friends and had to leave something wonderful and fruitful and satisfying.

On the other hand, you need to remember that you're leaving those friends and family members only in the physical sense. You're going to depend upon their prayers. You'll need them as "outsiders" who can offer a shoulder to cry on when it's impossible to vent your emotions around church members. You'll certainly need a foundation of financial support in the beginning. Even people who can send no more than five dollars per month have a place in your ministry, and their reliability will provide ongoing encouragement.

Some people leave to plant a church because things haven't gone well somewhere else. Maybe there are staff or congregational problems in the church they've been serving. It's surely an easy fantasy for troubled leaders: *If I could just go to some other part of the country, some place where people don't know me, and start all over again* ... Fantasies are very convenient, because in them, people behave the way we want them to behave. Real-world problems don't arise. Happy endings are guaranteed.

Yet a leading indicator of your future church success is your present success. If things are going well, your gifts are blessing the body of Christ, and *then* you feel a call, that's a good sign. You can pull your support circle together and celebrate that God is opening the next phase of an already fruitful ministry. Planting a church should never be a way of running away from disappointment. Amy and I counsel prospective pastors to make sure they are running *to* something instead of *from* something.

4. What Specific Thing about Church Planting Captures Your Imagination?

This is a very revealing question. We've talked to people who say, "I just love the idea of being unshackled from church traditions. I want to start a church so that we can build it the right way from the ground up." These are understandable sentiments, but they're not the right motives for building a new church; in fact, they represent just another fantasy of escape. Some are attracted to the idea of creativity, certain kinds of music and presentation, certain clothing, even the romantic idea of meeting in a school or movie theater. Their minds are fixed on Sunday morning, and they believe they can put together a powerful and creative worship service. Alas, church isn't confined to the morning worship service. It is ministry. It is relationship. It is a whole host of things that aren't showy or theatrical.

Others want to start a church because they're excited about the church-planting models they've seen. They want to enlist in a movement. Still others might simply be captivated by the adventure of the idea; they've heard the stories of how churches were built, and they want a legacy of building something for God from the ground up.

None of these attractions are bad in themselves, but please consider this: the draw of planting must come from a desire to reach people for Christ, with the conviction that this is the best way to do it, as well as the way God wants it done. If the big idea in your head is a specific model of worship service, then that's where your energies will go, and people will know it. If your big idea is the life of adventure, you'll struggle with your commitment the first time you realize there's a great deal of drudgery involved.

God's heart is for lost and hurting people. It's not about trendy styles of worship, the fun of the experience, or anything else. He grieves for his lost children in every community, on every street, and he wants a personal relationship with them. <u>Churches are planted as rescue missions to bring people into a relationship with Christ.</u> As a matter of fact, we are constantly telling our members —and church planters—that we want them to feel a sense of ownership over the lostness of their communities.

Vocation to Location

As you pray about your call, first seek confirmation that this is definitely what God wants you to do. That's the first and crucial step. Then look for a bond with the place where he wants you to go. In the same way that our hearts quickly opened to Paulding County, you will know when you've come to journey's end, the place where God has appointed you as a missionary.

You must bond with your vocation, but also with your location. You must feel a deep burden for its people. The Gospels often tell us that Jesus looked at the people and felt compassion for them, seeing them as sheep without a shepherd. You should see your people that way, with the emotions of Jesus, rather than as cold demographic data or as opportunities for you to show your stuff.

If you've felt drawn to this idea for one of the lesser motives above, then you need to keep praying and seeking the mind of Christ about your future. We can't say enough to discourage people from planting a church for the wrong reason.

On the other hand:

If you are deeply humbled by the idea that God could use you to reach lost people in spite of yourself ...

If the fingerprints of God are all over your circumstances, and you're becoming desperate to see him do the things that only he can do ...

If you couldn't care less whether anyone ever knows your name ...

If you have received confirmation and counsel from a
    spiritual mentor who has validated your leadership and
    your calling . . .

If you are ready to work harder than you've ever worked in
    your life . . .

If you are ready for spiritual warfare at a level you've never
    experienced . . .

If your spouse and family share the same vision to plant a
    church . . .

If you consider yourself tough-minded, resilient, and capable
    of hard decisions . . .

If the desire of your heart is seeing lost people come to
    Christ . . .

Then welcome to the wild and wonderful world of church
planting!

CHAPTER 3

HOW DO YOU LAUNCH A HEALTHY CHURCH?

Welcome to the Jungle

We'll always be grateful for Dr. Falwell's great heart and generosity. He allowed us to stay on staff for a year while we laid the foundation for our future church. Other than our parents and Dr. Falwell, we did not personally know anyone who had started a church, so we really valued Rick Warren's *The Purpose Driven Church*. It became our first church-planting manual. We gathered a small team of friends who shared our vision and were prepared to move with us. We wrote letters to almost everyone we knew, asking for prayer and financial support, and we kept in touch with my brother and sister-in-law, learning what we could about our target community.

We left Thomas Road Baptist Church in the height of our ministry, during what turned out to be our best year. Our seventh-grade class had introduced Amy and me to each other, since she was a schoolteacher for that age while I was a student minister. We had promised these kids that we'd stay in student ministry with them until they graduated. So the day after their graduation, a bunch of our students formed an assembly line in our front yard and packed our U-Haul. On June 1, 1997, we said our goodbyes to the friends and families who had been so important to us. It was difficult to believe that an era of our life was coming to an end. Stepping out of our comfort zone was both exciting and terrifying.

Everything we owned was loaded into the truck, which I drove. Amy and our two-year-old son, Taylor, followed in our car. We said a prayer for safe travel, and just like that, our still-unsold house became a shrinking image in our rearview mirrors.

We had rented a modest apartment in Lithia Springs, just south of Paulding County. After we made the drive of nearly five hundred miles, we began carrying all our possessions up to the second floor, where our new home was located. It was hot, humid, and the boxes felt heavy after a long drive. By the time Amy and I finished struggling to push our washing machine up the stairs, we were looking at each other and saying, "What in the world are we doing here?" It was one of those moments when you must decide whether to laugh or cry. We chose to laugh.

Our planting team included Steve and Christie Veale, from Boca Raton, Florida; Dave and Chris Cole, from Kansas City, Missouri; and Paul and Angela Richardson, from Lynchburg. These couples had left their jobs, sold their homes, and come with us to do something significant for the kingdom of God. Like Amy and me, they had spent many months raising their own financial support, so we all knew the meaning of sacrifice. The dream, of course, was that someday we would all draw regular salaries from a growing church. For now, however, we operated on faith and the loving help of our friends.

Days of Desperation

Amy, Taylor, and I spent about a month just making sure we were healthy. Our marriage was solid, and our son seemed to be adjusting in his new environment. We knew this was a time of spiritual preparation, when God would work on the soil of our hearts as much as the soil of our mission field. I remember sitting out on our apartment deck, reading, praying, and journaling. We had a deep sense of thrilled expectation about what God would soon begin.

We found ourselves desperate for God in a way we had never experienced before. If anything was going to happen, it would be through his power, strength, and wisdom, and not through any human capacity we were bringing to the table.

The sculptor Michelangelo used to carefully select a block of marble from the stone quarry. He knew that no block of stone would be perfect, no matter how meticulous he was. Each one had flaws. But he had a strong image in his mind of what he intended to carve out of that stone. Someone asked him, "How do you do that? How do you get from that big chunk of rock to the beautiful figure you're creating?"

He replied, "Well, I happen to be sculpting the figure of an angel. I see this angel trapped within the block. Then I begin chiseling away at it, month after month, scraping away everything that is not the angel." I felt that this was what God was doing to me — scraping away the old to make something new. The chiseling and scraping could be very painful. I read from the Scriptures and from books through which God spoke to me and showed me the changes that would be necessary. I wasn't particularly seeking information about leadership and church planting, though I love reading books on those subjects. This time was more about knowing God more intimately and laying myself bare before him.

The silence of the first Georgia days was a little unnerving. In Lynchburg, of course, our phone had been constantly ringing. We'd been surrounded by a community there. Now no one called. We realized what it meant to come into a new place where we knew almost no one — just a few people other than my brother Kevin; his wife, Dawn; and our little team. In a sense, we were on an island. We were explorers of a new world.

From time to time, we would check in with our Realtor to see what was happening with our house back in Lynchburg. Anyone looking at it? Any serious offers? Four months went by before the house sold, and during that time we lost all our equity in it, approximately twenty-four thousand dollars; after that, we had to pay two thousand dollars just to get rid of the house. That hurt, but we understood deep down that God was still sculpting, still creating something new. He wanted to know what mattered most to us — what we had saved or what he was planning. We just needed to trust his heart.

An even greater test came through the issue of our financial support. We had put a good deal of work into raising our support before our move to Georgia, writing hundreds of letters, and a number of people had made commitments. Now that we had made the trip and laid everything on the line, some of these commitments weren't panning out. As a matter of fact, some of the ones that fell away happened to be some of our biggest commitments and the ones we felt we could count on the most.

One day I called the supporter who had made the largest commitment and asked him for a final decision on whether he was going to come through for us. "I'm sorry," he said. "It's just not going to happen." I put down the phone, changed into my swimsuit, went down to our apartment pool, and feverishly swam laps. As I swam, I poured out my heart to God, saying, *God, we've lost all of our equity, we've emptied our savings, and now we've lost our biggest donor. I just can't seem to make sense of all this.* Somewhere in the midst of so much seeming misfortune, I felt a peace come over me, as if God were saying, *It's going to be all right. I didn't bring you and your family all this way to leave you hanging. You can't see how all of this is going to work out, but when it does, no one will be able to get the glory except me.*

It was in that pool that I knew God would somehow come through for us. I made a commitment to him that he would always get the glory. It was such an amazing lesson in faith for us. We had worked so hard to raise our support, and it didn't work quite as smoothly as we had anticipated. The ones we thought were most solid often disappointed us. Yet at the same time a great deal of support came from unexpected sources—faithful people who gave only a few dollars a month. God raised up significant partners in people we didn't even know. I've mentioned that Johnny Hunt, a pastor I hadn't met, came to me to offer his church's support. We had no idea before coming to this area that First Baptist of Woodstock would become our mother church, but what a wonderful resource that congregation became for us.

We understood that people who have served God through the years have spent time in the wilderness first, in times of strengthening and increased focus and dependence. It's God's pattern, and it was even required of Jesus. When things are too smooth, too easy, that's when we really need to worry. We understood this, but we were coming to a point of desperation—which usually means God has us exactly where he wants us.

"Sitemares"

No matter how much you prepare, your church plant will never go according to script. It's messy, unpredictable, and basically a voyage into the uncharted waters of a new community. During those first months, our team walked through neighborhoods knocking on doors and telling people about our new church. Taylor rode on my shoulders and helped us make friends. We also set up tables at several of our county's arts and crafts festivals, handing out free balloons to children. The balloons allowed us to meet families and tell them about our new church. Our goal was to create a buzz of excitement about West Ridge.

It was during these early days that we met six or seven families that had come out of a church split. Many of them were wounded, of course, nursing the unique hurts that result from a divided congregation. One of our first big questions was how to handle that group. Could they become the nucleus of the new church we wanted to build? There's such an eagerness in the beginning to find that initial core group of people. We really loved them, and they responded to us.

The problem was that they were a tight group with their own idea of what a new church should be like. They wanted to hear me bring a kind of "trial" sermon, after which they'd decide whether to call me as their pastor. Of course, that wasn't the scenario we had in mind. We wanted to start a church rather than be added to one. We had brought our own vision of what was to be built, and we simply couldn't compromise it at the outset in order to gain a handful of charter members.

We met in a small Methodist church for several weeks on Thursday evenings during that summer, the core leaders plus anyone interested. We talked about our vision and values, and we reviewed our prospectus. But we also confronted our first site issue. One night we found a woman waiting for us on the front porch of the church. She said, "You can't meet here anymore."

We said, "But we have an agreement with the pastor. We're paying for the use of the space, and—"

"The pastor doesn't run this church. I do."

She told us we could have one more evening to meet in the building. So our focus shifted toward finding another place to meet. We went to every school in the area, to a restaurant, even to a tire store. *Where to now, God? You brought us here, so ... where?* At this point a friend named Ike Reighard, who had started a church in Kennesaw just up the road, gave me a call. Ike was another man God sent to help steer us through tough times. His church donated chairs, his staff hung out with us, and he became a valuable mentor.

Ike directed us to Vaughn Elementary School. Vaughn, not too far away from us, was in Cobb County. We were hesitant because we felt the site needed to be in Paulding. Georgia, by the way, has more counties than any other state in the union other than

Texas, and sometimes county lines become an issue with people. As a matter of fact, we were told early on that people from Cobb County would not cross into Paulding to go to church.

I explained our intentions to Ike. He said, "I understand where you'd like to be, but I don't see how you have any other options." He was right. There was no other place available to us. Amy called the office in charge of the facility to ask about using it. She was told we might as well be asking for the moon. "There's a three-to-five-year waiting list," said the woman. "It's not going to happen."

Nevertheless, we put in our request and even made it extensive. We asked for the cafeteria, gymnasium, and classroom usage. If you're asking for the moon, go for the whole thing. The next morning the woman called back. She said, "I've been working for the county for eighteen years, and I've never seen anything like this. You got everything you asked for."

Suddenly our church had a home.

When it comes to relationships with the community, I (Ike) remember Zig Ziglar saying that if you will help other people get out of life what they want out of life, people are going to help you get what you want out of life. You never use that as a manipulation but as a philosophy. If God's given me a gift, it is that I love people. Inspiration means that you breathe life into people. I can't give someone a dream, but I can breathe life into theirs. I call it doing ministry with no strings attached. We just say, "How can I help you?" You go in and you find the needs in schools and around the community and find how you can make it better. When you start serving like that, it's amazing how it will turn out good for you. Be friends with people, and encourage them.

— Ike and Robin Reighard,
Piedmont Baptist Church, Marietta, GA

Maiden Voyage

We continued to knock on doors, inviting people to come to the new West Ridge Church that would open in the fall. We handed them a brochure my sister-in-law had created on her computer, and during the final days of preparation, we brought in college students from Lexington, Kentucky, who knocked on two thousand more doors, making sure everyone had gotten word about the new church start-up.

On September 7 we held our first church service. I hardly slept on Saturday night, and I felt sick to my stomach as I climbed out of bed. I knew I should be excited and filled with praise and expectation, but I was shot through with anxiety. What if no one showed up? Well, I knew that at least Amy and Taylor would be there; she had given me her promise, with a big smile, the night before. Thanks, Amy!

But what about our core group of hurting people—were they truly in our corner? What about all the hours knocking on doors, handing out brochures? Amy and I prayed hard that God would pull people out of bed and send them our way.

As I drove up Highway 278, I was thinking in terms of somewhere to pull over and lose my breakfast. I managed to avoid that, however, and I arrived at the church. As I walked into the room, everything was in place—including 251 people who watched with expectant eyes. We were overwhelmed. It was a good place to start.

For our first service, we had hired a band from Nashville, not knowing where else to find musicians. The band, with its long hair and guitars, led us in "Celebrate Jesus, Celebrate." I had asked them to make a musical statement about the kind of church we were going to be. But the moment they began to play, a large group of people stood up and walked out. The woman who had brought most of these people wrote us a letter that said, with more than a touch of sarcasm, "Thank you for my first rock concert."

It was something different for the average local church attender. There was no choir, and there were no hymnals. The pastor and staff were dressed comfortably, no ties or suits. We didn't use the King James Version; we used the more contemporary New American Standard Version. In 1997, these things were brand-new to Paulding County. Most churches looked and felt much as they had for half a century or more. We were shocked to start hearing around the community that we were thought of as a cult. Some of the leaders of the local churches weren't too excited to have us as neighbors. One pastor even walked into my office and challenged me and our staff to a fistfight!

At least the phone had started ringing. There was a certain amount of tension, but we knew we were going to stick it out — even though we began to feel like "the incredible shrinking church." On week 2, after many of our friends and relatives went home, and the churched crowd realized I wasn't Jerry Falwell, our attendance settled in at 140.

We were totally unprepared for the emotional low that hit us after all the excitement of launch Sunday had come and gone. An even harder lesson came as our numbers seemed to dip a bit more each week until bottoming out at 98 on the Sunday after Christmas.

Learning to Trust

We tried not to think too much about numbers and attendance and to keep our focus on the fact that people were coming to know the Lord each week. We felt a true calling to what we were doing, and that meant that we put our faith in God rather than attendance charts. We set our salaries at the survival level, kept inviting people, kept ministering to the people who honored us with their presence, and remembered that friends and family were praying — and sometimes paying — for every day.

Many of them were giving sacrificially too. We had written people from every stage of our lives, friends from elementary school through college, friends from ministry, and members of extended family, and they had committed to help us for two years, financially and with daily prayer. This only increased our desire to stick it out, to serve God to the best of our ability, and to validate the trust those friends and family members had placed in us.

We had a post office box at a local shipping center, and we visited it day by day, hoping the funding would appear in that box so we could go another week. I remember a day when we were fighting discouragement. We had just seen our lowest attendance and lowest offering yet. I still have that day's small deposit slip in the top drawer of my desk, a reminder of a tough moment. I said to Amy, "Let's pray all day long."

I talked to God, asking him if his hand was still upon us, whether he still wanted us to keep after this thing, and whether he had some idea for us other than West Ridge Church. We had counted the cost, but perhaps we hadn't counted on that cost continuing to rise. When I got to our post office box, I opened the door and found a couple of small checks — one for forty dollars, one for sixty — and concentrated on thanking God for the donations, knowing they were not enough to meet our staff payroll.

We got through Christmas and realized we had come to the tipping point. Our funds were depleted. As much as we struggled to keep our costs low, we had three staff families and one part-timer to support. It takes money to make a church happen, and our cupboard was bare. We had exactly $22.21 in our church bank account. Our worship pastor, Steve, and I painted a house for three weeks just to have money for Christmas presents.

Our church office was the basement of the home of a staff member's parents. I sat in that basement fighting discouragement on the afternoon of New Year's Eve. It was what Henry Blackaby describes as a "crisis of belief." We were working hard, praying, but wondering what lay ahead for us in 1998. As I drove home that afternoon, my cell phone rang. It was an older gentleman who had become a dear friend. He was a very active member of a large church nearby, and he asked if I could come by his house. I agreed to meet with him; then I turned my car around and called Amy to tell her I'd be a little late.

When I arrived at his home, he greeted me and came right to the point. "Two of my daughters and their families have been attending your church."

"Yes, sir," I said, bracing for a complaint about the music or my not wearing a suit and tie.

"I want you to know that we believe in what you're doing."

"Yes, sir?"

"I love my daughters, and I see the difference in their lives — how excited they are about the church."

"Thank you, sir," I said with a smile and a sigh of relief.

"Now, if you put in just a few more hymns, we might attend more often ourselves," he said, grinning. He reached for an envelope and handed it to me. "I've been blessed through my business," he said, "and I want you to have this."

I thanked him again. I never know whether I'm supposed to open a gift envelope immediately or wait discreetly until later. "Go ahead," he urged. "Open it!"

So I did. It contained a check for thirty thousand dollars.

What could I say? How could I respond? I wept. I couldn't have done anything else. He cried too, and so did his wife.

I had never experienced anything like that. If life as a planter had been easy and comfortable, I would have been robbed of the blessing of having God meet my needs in such a beautiful and timely way. God was saying, *Are you getting it now? I still believe in you, so you just keep believing in me. I will never forsake you. Are you hearing that? Never!*

Why is this thing so personal? Because God meets your needs

in a highly personal way. He requires you to come up close, to push your faith to a new and uncomfortable level. And the greater your need, the greater your joy when he meets it — and the greater he is glorified.

I suppose I didn't touch the ground on the way out to the car, but I had to pull the car over because I could not see to drive for the tears in my eyes. I put my head down on the steering wheel. "God," I prayed, "I will never doubt again what you are doing with this church." I wish I could say I've completely lived up to that goal.

It was a happy new year! Our little team met and made a valuable decision. We were going to honor God by tithing on that donation. We took three thousand dollars and started a church in India. And God showed up again and did some more spectacular things through that decision.

But that's a story for another chapter.

Questions to Think About

1. Are You Clear about What Kind of Church God Wants You to Plant?

Church planting is such a high-stakes challenge that people who attempt it will do almost anything to succeed. And there's a great deal of danger in that situation. For example, new churches tend to attract disgruntled ex-members of other churches. They often arrive as close-knit factions, and they see the new church as the perfect place to unpack their agenda. That young pastor will surely be easier to influence than the stubborn, experienced one they've just left behind.

As the church planter, therefore, you must confront the question of whether you're willing to hold to the vision you've followed to this point. I can remember a number of occasions when we were invited to friendly dinners that inevitably came to the real point: Would we do this or that in our new church, and would we let them be the leaders of it? Would we have a particular kind of music and feature tonight's hostess as a soloist?

It's so tempting to try to make everyone's dream come true, particularly when you're struggling to build a new church — "You scratch my back (by joining) and I'll scratch yours (by giving you what you want)." But once you begin making compromises, you're no longer following a vision; you're following a political course. We learned to be very clear about what kind of church we were building, and we graciously said no on any number of occasions. The smiles often froze on our hosts' faces at that point; dinner was over, and forget dessert.

Sometimes we may appear rigid and inflexible about our plans, but it simply doesn't work to allow all comers to vote on what the church can become. We're building a unified, focused body of Christ whose vision is to see people changed by the gospel; we can't let people change the vision with their own agenda. We heard that people were referring to that song about the Devil going down to Georgia and saying that it was written about *me*. You have to have thick skin to hold firm to a God-given vision.

During our first week, when so many people walked out, we could have run after them and promised to change our music. When they insisted on a certain style of preaching or dress, we could have put these things up for a vote. I'm convinced that if we had done that, we'd have had better numbers to begin with, and almost no future at all.

2. Have You Counted the Cost? And Are You Willing to Do What It Takes in the Attempt to Plant Your Church?

I've described how, at the very outset, we told Mac Riggs we were willing to face a future of flipping burgers; we were going to see this church work or die trying. In the great rush to plant churches today, I'm not certain everyone has considered the high price they might be asked to pay. Sometimes it's the grace of God that we don't know our own future and how low the lows might be. On the other hand, Jesus had a lot to say about picking up one's cross and following him. We need to count the cost. We need to be well informed that church planting is not an easy life.

Peter the disciple stepped out of the boat on Jesus's invitation. His one mistake was that he looked down. Church planting is a faith exercise in stepping out of the boat. If you keep your eyes on Jesus, everything will be all right. Gravity will set in only if you give it permission to override your faith.

At least Peter took that step from the boat. We took our step, and we knew that if we looked down, the waves would swallow us. But as we told Mac, we knew Jesus would love us even if we failed to keep our heads above the surface. We knew he would always reach down, pull us up, and give us something else to do. But we understood we were laying a great deal on the line.

3. Are You Willing to Do the Tough Work to Take People on a Spiritual Journey?

The most thrilling week of church planting is week 1. The least thrilling is week 2. Once the adrenaline rush of that first worship gathering is over, reality sets in. There are rows and rows of folding chairs to put away—and next week you'll do it all again! Long after the guests shake your hand and go home, you'll be down on the floor cleaning coffee stains off the rented facility's carpet.

When we were meeting at a high school during a certain period, we had a special team that arrived early to paint over offensive language on the stalls of the restroom. During the school week, the words always came back, and so did our workers.

Church planting is relentlessly *daily*. We feel the lure of that creative worship service, of the newness of everything. But it's the difference between a wedding ceremony and a marriage—you've got to be in it for the long haul. The service lasts an hour, and then the real ministry begins; the problems begin to multiply. I remember pulling one or two checks out of our post office box and realizing that tomorrow I would be right here again, and the needs would be even greater. You're going to need to trust God one day at a time.

In the long run, it's really not about buildings or music or marketing. It's about the power of the gospel. It's about the down-and-dirty work of getting into people's lives and problems. For Jesus, it was about touching lepers, going to the homes of social outcasts. For you, the church planter, it won't be much different. If you open a church in the name of Christ, and if you're serious about that, then Jesus is going to send the people he wants you to love and care for. Some of them will present problems. It's going to be messy, even painful. It won't look a thing like the glamorous daydreams you once had of starting a church.

But the rewards are very significant. You will experience God in a way you never have before. You will see life-changing miracles firsthand. To be used by God is one of the greatest honors and joys available to us.

4. Are You Willing to Be Broken and Prepared?

If you really plan to take on this challenge, then *welcome to the jungle*! You're en route to the mysterious regions that lie outside your comfort zone. Church planting will expose every weakness in you. It will bring every flaw to the surface and put it on public display. Check your pride at the door.

Since you are going to the front line of ministry, you can expect to see some military action. There will be spiritual warfare on a level that occurs only where Satan is desperate not to lose ground. Know this too: he doesn't fight fair. He will find your most vulnerable spots, having probed all the seams of your character, looking for a weak place. If not there, he will attack your marriage;

if not your marriage, you can look for him to turn up in parenting situations.

In other words, this time it's personal.

My fear is that too many prospective church planters are hurrying past the training ground that is so crucial to their endurance, rushing in. Younger people are doing much of the planting, and their energy is an asset; however, it is essential that they are ready and prepared.

I learned so much under my first pastor, John Hibbard, who taught me how to shepherd people and lead a church through tough times. I learned from Dr. Falwell how to cast a vision and deal with conflict. During my apprenticeship under these men, I had the opportunity to make my mistakes "under someone else's umbrella." I had the opportunity to fail and to learn from failure, without so much at stake. The days of the launch will create memories you'll have forever — some of them painful, some of them wonderful, all of them representing the work of God, who is sculpting an amazing church even as he sculpts your character.

CHAPTER 4

HOW DO YOU PROTECT YOUR MARRIAGE WHILE PLANTING A CHURCH?

Beware of Collateral Damage

I'm tightly wired, and I doubt I'm the only church leader who is that way.

I was once an extreme workaholic. I was determined to be the first one into the office in the morning, the last one to leave at night. I never thought in terms of hours per week; I just knew that I had goals and I was in a mad rush to reach them. I had been a college athlete, so I was driven, competitive, and finish-line oriented. And who was going to tell me I should stop trying to do my best?

Before I met Amy, I had been engaged to another young lady. My fiancée let me know she was unhappy with the level of my attachment to work. She questioned whether my attachment to her was anywhere close to being as strong. I shared this conflict with a friend who had been in ministry for many years. He was concerned about my fiancée's understanding of things. He said, "You need to help her see that ministry must come first. We're serving God, and marriage has to fit into that."

At the time, I confess, this seemed like wise advice. It represented the priority scale in many churches: give 100 percent to the kingdom of God, and let God sort out the rest of the stuff in your life; you trust him, and he'll fill in the gaps. Now I see that as a very dangerous misunderstanding. I also see a lot of eager church planters falling into the same trap.

Amy and I began dating in September of 1991. She was a seventh-grade teacher while I was a student pastor. Not only was I putting in a lot of time, but I was working a very unstructured schedule. Anyone who has been in student ministry knows how this can go. The students had regular activities to be created and maintained for Sunday mornings, Sunday evenings, and Wednesday evenings. Nearly every weekend brought some kind of special event. We also sponsored ministry teams that traveled to detention centers and churches on weekends, or even weeknights, to perform martial arts, gymnastics, drama, and music. Leading a vigorous student ministry is plenty of work for the ordinary student pastor. But I wanted even more, so I volunteered as a football and baseball coach at a high school nearby. Oh, and there was also my work toward earning a master's degree at seminary.

Once I met Amy, I felt it was a perfect fit: we both worked with students, and many of the same students. That allowed me to kill two birds with one stone, since I could get in a lot of "dating" while we were at student events. Very efficient!

No, that wasn't fair, but we were young and in love, and togetherness was enough for us at that point. Besides, Amy is a very special human being. She has terrific people skills, is devoted to serving Christ, and I would have been as blind as a bat not to see that God had sent a once-in-a-lifetime blessing my way. So we were engaged and then married. I figured we'd return from our honeymoon and pick up right where we left off, ministry and marriage and no real boundary between them. I expected her to keep working as a full-time teacher, then be there for all my student activities during her time off.

I had every Monday as a day off to rest a bit. But Amy worked a normal Monday-to-Friday schedule, including grading papers and other off-hour responsibilities. Therefore she would go hard through the workweek, join me in the middle of some big Saturday student ministry event, and then it would be a full day of church on Sunday, morning to late evening. I had plenty of energy, and I figured that if I put God's work first, he would make everything in my life work somehow. Boundaries? I didn't know what those were.

One night, after about a year of marriage, we were returning home from some evening event when Amy's battery simply ran out. We were coming in the door, and she collapsed in my arms. After I lowered her to the sofa, I could see that she was too exhausted to stand up again. She began to cry and couldn't stop. I just stood there and felt helpless.

"Brian," she said, "I can't keep this up. I can't continue to go and go and go." Worse, she felt guilty about those limitations. "I feel so weak. And I'm mad at myself for not being stronger, not being able to do everything."

"Well," I said, in all my fumbling ability to be understanding, "I guess you just don't have the passion for students that I do."

Yes, I said that. Even as the words were coming out of my mouth, I wished I could have reeled them back in. But I said the words, and she was devastated. Amazingly, I had sincerely thought I was right in tune with Amy's feelings and desires at the time. Maybe I had believed that I was becoming Super Pastor and that she was happily holding on to my cape as we soared through the world of ministry. But now I could look at her, collapsed on that sofa, and see that she had passed her limit. It had nothing to do with passion for students; she needed a break.

I'd love to say that we changed everything overnight. It took some time for me to figure out how to manage my life, my ministry, and my marriage. But this was a turning point, and God began to help me see that I couldn't delegate the management of my family to him; he expected me to get my own priorities in order.

Today we've made that terrible evening into a kind of symbol of the worst that can happen when we don't value rest. If we're leaning toward overcommitment and burnout, Amy looks at me and says, "Remember that little place I get to, at the end of my rope?"

I know that place well, and we don't go there.

> So much of our dating relationship was about me (Pete) pursuing her, but then we got married and I had a new challenge, starting the church. All of my attention shifted to the church. I assumed that because we were in love, our relationship would take care of itself. It was several years until I realized that if our marriage was going to be healthy and grow, we would have to be as intentional about it as we were with the church.
>
> I (Brandi) allowed the church to be first, and I felt like I was being selfish because Pete was working for the Lord and bringing people to Christ. This is what I had chosen to give up, but our marriage can become like a business. I am so independent that Pete said that the only thing I needed him for was to pay the bills. We have been to counseling a few times in our marriage, and our counselor told us that having needs does not make me needy.
>
> — Pete and Brandi Wilson,
> Cross Point Church, Nashville, TN

A Marathon, Not a Sprint

One of the things that first attracted me (Amy) to Brian was his passion for serving God. When we got married, there was no question that I bought into it. If I didn't like working with students, I would never have gone into teaching. But I couldn't do everything. And even though I was healthy and energetic, I couldn't keep up a nonstop pace seven days a week. When the mad rush began to take its toll, I felt guilty about resenting it, about wanting more of Brian and more time to ourselves. The last thing I wanted was to be the weak link in his ministry.

I can remember rising early on Monday to start a new week after a busy weekend of church activities. Brian was resting and recharging a bit — not that he spent much time relaxing. But dragging out the door to school on another Monday morning, I coveted his day off. I was starting to realize I had hit the wall; I had come to my limit.

But what was there to do? No one at the office was going to tell Brian to slow down, to give a little more time to his marriage. When he suggested that I lacked his passion for students, I didn't hit him with a frying pan; I just felt misunderstood. And I wondered if he was right. But after that night, I could see him becoming more sensitive to my plight. He realized that I didn't need to be Wonder Wife to his Super Pastor. Things began to improve, even though when our son Taylor came along, he got pulled right into the rat race. We took him to every event, every responsibility, and he spent his first couple of years thinking he was a teenager himself.

Today Brian and I have both learned the importance of setting careful boundaries and making them known. We have come to understand that this is a marathon, not a sprint. He protects me and my time, and disciplines himself to work at a healthy pace as well. I love him for that. Best of all, no one on his staff is going to overdo it if Brian finds out about it. He likes to say that when you spend too much time away from home, someone is suffering for it. And if you don't establish clear boundaries, you are setting yourself up for disaster and burnout.

The Nature of the Beast

One of the hard things about ministry is that it's not a nine-to-five job. You never punch the clock and go home with a sense of being totally caught up. There's always something else you could have done, and there's always someone who is disappointed with something. For church planters in particular, the demands are constant and open ended. The planter is doing everything for an understaffed start-up. He is constantly reassuring himself and his spouse, "It won't be this way forever; this is just for now." But while he burns the candle at both ends, he sets a pattern that will endure and will eventually consume him from the inside. Ministry isn't only time-consuming; it's *all*-consuming.

We've shared our story with many church-planting couples over nearly two decades of our marriage. They've shared theirs too. I (Brian) can't tell you how many times we've seen these people sigh, take off their masks, and reveal just how frustrated and miserable they are under the facade of pastoral well-being. Today's church planter talks about the incredible, unending stress, the ongoing criticism and potshots, the pressure of financing, the grind of sermon preparation, and the general feeling that he lives in a fishbowl with no place to run and hide. He has problems with blood pressure, and usually he cannot sleep, because his mind will not shut down. As for his wife, she is so upset she can't even talk about it, except for her desire to toss his smartphone into the garbage. She usually mentions that she has always felt she needed to "take one for the team."

As we have these conversations with young couples, the tears will begin to glisten in the planter's eyes and in the eyes of his wife as he says, "I want to slow down, pull back, ease off. I want to take better care of her, but I don't know how to make that happen. I don't want anyone to accuse me of being lazy."

Choosing to Cheat

My true turning point came in the year 2000, when I had lunch with Andy Stanley, senior pastor of Northpoint Church in Alpharetta, Georgia. I was an admirer of his leadership and the way he handles himself in ministry, and I looked forward to spending a little time with him. On most such occasions, I would have brought six or seven burning questions to ask. But this time, I had only one—and it was a big one.

I was at a crossroads and I knew it. Just as Amy had once realized she was hitting the wall, now it was my turn. After all those early months of struggle, suddenly it was all happening at West Ridge Church. We were approaching the one thousand milestone in weekly attendance, and I was more on the run than ever. I knew Andy had grown up in a large church and had now built one he was leading.

My question for him was, "How can I pastor a large, growing church without losing my marriage and my family?" I explained that Amy and I are both very driven people. We'd poured everything we had into getting this church off the ground. We were beginning to feel overwhelmed. It was starting to impact our home life.

His answer rocked my world. Andy looked at me and said, "You have to choose to cheat."

I was perplexed. "What does that mean?"

"The church wants all of you. Your family *needs* all of you. You've got to cheat one or the other, so you must give yourself permission to choose to cheat the church, then refuse to cheat your family."

"But ..."

He explained to me that if I were to lose my family, I would lose my ministry as well. I could always dial back my work hours, but I couldn't afford to dial back family time. God gave that to us as our first priority. Jesus said *he* would build his church, but he leaves it up to us to build our families.

It all sounded great. But it was so counterintuitive to what I had always understood about discipleship and ministry. I had always thought that because I was in full-time ministry, God would take care of my marriage and my kids. After all, I was doing his work.

I was realizing now that there's nothing spiritual or godly about workaholism. As a matter of fact, it's one more form of idolatry.

As Andy unpacked this concept before me, he made one statement that particularly undermined my old way of thinking: "God never promises to make up for misguided priorities." I realized my view that God would fill in the gaps was some pretty sloppy theology.

Andy saw that he was blowing my mind, and he smiled. "Did you know I just spoke about this last Sunday?" he asked. "Follow me back to my office, and I'll give you a tape of the message." On the way home, I pushed in that tape, listened to Andy speak, and fought tears. For the first time, I had been given permission to put my family before my ministry. Heresy? No—good common sense. It was so logical. The God I knew didn't want me to neglect my wife and my children. He is the ultimate, infinite model of an attentive father. Not only that, but all those years, as I had lived by the mythology of overwork, there had been evidence right in front of my nose that I had it wrong. I had been seeing hardworking, ministry-first men and women with crumbling marriages and rebellious children.

A few weeks later I played that tape for our elders during a retreat in the Georgia mountains. As they listened, many of them teared up just as I had. Most of them were business and community leaders. I realized that this isn't just about ministry; this is a cultural phenomenon. In our nation, as families come apart at the seams and as massive numbers of people fight depression, we need to reevaluate our relationships to work and to family. We need to think again about whom we can and cannot afford to cheat.

Significant decisions came out of that retreat in Blue Ridge, Georgia. There was a time of repentance and rededication to our marriages and our children. We decided to limit the workweek at West Ridge to forty-five hours, though there occasionally could be exceptions. If we couldn't get certain jobs done, we would hire people or enlist new volunteers to fill in the gaps. It was one of the great turning points of my life, and I am passionate about helping planters, pastors, and career people everywhere learn the same lesson.

Marriage, I believe, is the most important ministry God has given you. If you're planting a church or considering planting one, it becomes all the more critical that you understand this. Therefore we want to offer you some very practical advice on how to set proper boundaries and live by them. Amy put this list together, and I think it's a great one.

1. Do What Is important, Not What Is Urgent

Brian and I learned long ago that it is too easy to attend to the immediate thing, the *noisy* need, rather than the most important one. We tend to be all over the place. We put out fires; we attend to whoever yells loudest. Then we're too exhausted to take care of the things that the still, small voice of God is telling us to do. Church planters live within the tension between the merely urgent and the truly important; the squeaky wheel gets too much of the grease.

We simply can't please all the people all the time, and that's a difficult truth for people pleasers like Brian and me. If you try to make everyone happy, the ones who lose out will be the ones you know will forgive you: your spouse and your children. But that's not fair to them, is it?

Your marriage and your family head your life priority list, and that doesn't change. Live as if you truly believe that. Figure out what your purpose is. Decide what it is that you do, and cut out everything else.

2. Bring Fun and Adventure into Your Relationship

When we got married, Brian and I wrote our own vows. We also used traditional vows, but we wanted to speak specifically to some issues that mattered to us. In Brian's vows to me, he promised that he would be in charge of *fun*. It made me grin to see him in a tuxedo, during a beautiful wedding ceremony, vowing to be a fun person. I loved it. It's true that he was very serious about work in those days, but he was "seriously fun," and that was one of the things that attracted me to him. Through the years, even in the toughest times, we have never forgotten to enjoy life. Brian likes to look at me and ask, "Amy, are we still having fun?"

I have read that when wives of pastors get involved in extramarital affairs, it tends to be because the other man was someone who was fun to be with. We simply can't let the joy drain out of our marriage. Sometimes Brian and I realize that we have become too much like business partners, and that scares us. We choose something fun or romantic to remind us that we are about much more than business and church. We try to get out of town together once or twice a year without our boys. As much as we adore our children, we know that we need some "just us" time. Maybe you feel that you or your children couldn't bear to be out of each other's sight. I would say that you need to get over it. And it just may be good for your children to have the experience of staying with a friend or relative.

We're big on celebrations in our family. Anything you can do to make everyday life more festive is good for your family. Laughter is a daily vitamin, a medicine, and a love potion all rolled into one. Our best advice is to remember how much fun you used to have together, and rekindle that flame. Choose to do something just for fun.

3. Take Time Off Every Week

This one is so important: *Take your day off.*

I know people mean well by working overtime. Sometimes it appears that you can't afford a day off; the truth is, it's the other way around. You can't afford not to take a day off. There's a reason why God modeled the concept of rest when he created this world.

Why would an all-powerful, untiring God take a day off? Because it's important to him for us to understand how he made us. In his book *Our God Is Awesome*, Tony Evans writes that God rested not because he was all sweaty and tired but because he chose to model for us the importance of rest.

Friday is Brian's day off. If you call us on that day, you're likely to get our voicemail. Where are we? Out to lunch (literally), washing the truck, catching a matinee. (We love it that lunch and an early movie make a good, cheap date!) In the beginning it was all we could do not to leap up and answer a ringing phone. We felt guilty and unresponsive. But we reminded ourselves that rest is a godly priority and that we do it not because we care any less about ministry but because we care enough about it to take care of ourselves for the long haul. As a result, we find that we enter those other six days with fully recharged batteries, and we're far more effective in what we do.

Rest — why didn't we think of it sooner?

4. Keep Intimacy a Priority

Like everything else, intimacy is a matter of priority.

I know it seems counterintuitive. Isn't love supposed to be spontaneous, romantic? Yes, of course, but in a busy world, you must plan, prioritize, and even schedule it. Planned intimacy may not sound like a movie on the Lifetime channel, but often women think of physical intimacy as a very important item on life's to-do list. It can get lost in a forest of demands: that the children be bathed, that the dinner dishes be washed, that the laundry be done.

We need to be proactive and learn how to keep that spark in marriage. One way is for the husband to help his wife with household duties. The four sexiest words a wife will ever hear are, "How can I help?" The kids need help with homework. The laundry needs to be folded. A little support frees up time, and it certainly doesn't hurt a wife's romantic feelings toward her husband.

Both husband and wife need to think of intimacy from the other's perspective. The wife needs to understand that there are times when she needs to forget the housework and the less important items on the to-do lists and initiate a time of intimacy with her husband. Let him know that he is your priority; he's going to respond well to that. Women are drawn to physical intimacy when they feel good about themselves, but oftentimes men desire that closeness when things are challenging in their lives. It helps simply to understand this and to see our physical intimacy through the eyes of our partner. A wife needs to know that after a hard day, her husband needs her love—regardless of whether she feels desirable or has had time to shave her legs. A husband needs to help his wife feel more attractive, to let her know that he still finds her just as wonderful and alluring as on the day they met. Remember that connecting emotionally is one of the most important forms of intimacy. If you lose that connection, physical intimacy tends to be put aside. Be sure you're communicating, listening, and empathizing with each other every day.

5. Focus on Being a Team

Early in marriage, Brian and I would talk about other couples we admired. It was the way they functioned together: they were a *team*. Brian would say, "Let's do that just as well. I want us to be a team." As an athlete and sports fan, he understood that concept thoroughly.

I wanted to say, "I thought we were already a team."

Nineteen years have passed, and now I feel confident in saying we're on the same roster; we know our strengths as a team. What factors have made the difference? Time, for one. Brian points out that when a football team trades for a player, the newcomer may not fit into the dynamic of the locker room immediately. He has to gel with the others, and that takes time. Newly married couples need to go through a lot of little things: bill paying, home maintenance, and of course parenting. If they don't function tightly as a team, parenting will be a disaster.

Crises can help to create that unity. When Brian's dad died in 2004, we knew we were facing our first real tragedy, and we had no choice but to pull together and help one another through that dark valley. We faced sad days and sleepless nights that no one else ever knew about. We turned to God and to each other in real desperation, and in time, though we still bitterly miss my father-in-law, we became a stronger couple through our perseverance in grief.

Teamwork begins with open communication. We can learn something from the skill of using a drive-through window at a fast-food restaurant. You need to clearly state exactly what you want and how you want it done, then listen as it's repeated back to you. Sadly, we often do that less well for marriage than for a cheeseburger. We need to spend much more time listening.

As for parenting, we find that we need to set our policies ahead of time, and out of our kids' hearing, so we can hold to them with a unified front when questions come up. Children, of course, will try to divide and conquer, deciding which parent is the soft touch and trying to leverage one against the other. Never let that happen. As a matter of fact, say the words to your kids. Say, "We're a team."

Teammates do so many things well. They have no secrets between one another. They pick each other up when one is stumbling. That's the kind of teamwork we're talking about.

6. Find Your Significance and Security in Christ

Church planting doesn't provide a great deal of job security. Your church can pass its tenth or its twentieth anniversary, and you still face moments of instability and crisis. Men tend to look for their significance in what they do for a living, so this is an important point: you won't find that sense of significance and security in church planting.

We were created, as human beings, to find our meaning not in what we do but in what God has done for us. He provides the significance and the deep feeling of security that even the best marriage, even the godliest work, can't provide. What happens otherwise? If the husband is the pastor, he comes home at dinnertime craving a shot of self-esteem. He's been taking a beating, and he wants his number one cheerleader to build him back up. But she's not too fresh herself—not after a day of household crises. As a matter of fact, she may be looking for her husband to perform a little overtime ministry. Both are needy, and neither is in shape to be the helping partner.

Both must learn to move through their days feeling the significance that only God can bring us. We need to allow the Spirit of God to fill us through the day so that instead of draining one another, we are free to give to one another. Not that we don't still need the comforts and support of this bond, but it's a fact that no matter how wonderful marriage is, the deepest spiritual needs cannot be met there. They can be met only in Christ, and when they are, husbands and wives become much more attractive to each other.

7. Make Time for Meaningful Communication

When Taylor was one year old, we left him with my parents overnight for the first time. We were taking a twenty-four-hour getaway, an exciting event for us. We made a deal that we wouldn't talk about our child for the duration of that trip, because it was time to focus on each other. You may know that the first year with a first child is a time when the couple's relationship can suddenly slide into obscurity. The child is the center of the parents' universe. We knew that, and we wanted to be sure we were still connecting.

As we sat down for dinner at Olive Garden, we congratulated ourselves, drank in our freedom — and realized we couldn't think of a single subject to talk about! Taylor and ministry had been our whole year; subtract those, and there wasn't much left.

How sad. That fact in itself became a topic for conversation. We decided it wouldn't happen again. Right through the strenuous course of our lives, we needed a steady diet of humor, books, current events, challenges, and spiritual topics to share between us. We needed a rich field of interests that had nothing to do with work or children.

What are your dreams? What are the fears that you can't discuss with anyone else? Get the conversation rolling, and keep that fire lit 24/7/365. Most of all, keep your ears unclogged — listen attentively.

8. *Help Your Spouse Go as Far as He or She Can Go*

I see myself as head cheerleader for my husband, and it makes me feel good to push him to new levels of accomplishment. He realizes he needs to do the same for me. Our marriage is not all about his ministry; it has a deep and wonderful life of its own. He works to keep me from being sucked into the all-encompassing craziness of a full church schedule so that I can be free to follow my own dreams and my personal sense of where God is leading me.

I ran cross-country in high school. I wasn't the fastest sprinter, but I could run for a long time. Sometimes runners strap small weights to their ankles so their legs will have to work harder, developing muscles that wouldn't be optimized otherwise. In races, of course, the weights come off and the feet seem to fly, they feel so light.

Compare this with what the Bible tells us: "Do you not know that in a race all the runners run, but only one gets the prize? Run in such a way as to get the prize" (1 Cor. 9:24). Life is a race, and God places us on teams. I picture myself running alongside Brian, and we're encouraging each other, straining toward that finish line. But I don't want to put those extra weights on him. My task is to help him in the actual race of life, to help him feel light and fast. He has that same task for me.

In marriage, it's far too easy for us to load each other down with so many hindrances and extra burdens that our steps become slower and we finally stumble. Our insecurity and negativity are weights. Our failure to find significance in Christ, demanding it from the relationship instead, is a weight. Chaos, busyness, discontentment — all weights.

"Let us throw off everything that hinders and the sin that so easily entangles. And let us run with perseverance the race marked out for us, fixing our eyes on Jesus, the pioneer and perfecter of faith" (Heb. 12:1 – 2). I love those New Testament verses about racing and competition. In my mind's eye, I can see the finish line. I see myself pressing toward it, but I also see Brian. I want to see the look of joy and victory on his face as he crosses it, knowing he has succeeded in the things God set out for him to do.

9. Share Your Spiritual Lives with Each Other

It's strange, isn't it? There are so many couples in ministry who walk with the Lord but not together. We've offered statistics that show how seldom pastors pray with their own wives. It's hard to imagine why this is true; though, in our experience, we've seen how challenging it can be to make that time.

The pastor shares his spiritual journey with a crowded worship center. He goes to Bible study meetings and opens up about his walk with God. Why can't he do the same in his own home, his own sanctuary? There might be several reasons.

- The pastor realizes his spouse knows him all too well. She has seen him at his most vulnerable and worst moments. It's much easier for him to "talk the talk" around people who aren't so up close and personal. He worries that his wife will think him a hypocrite.

- Husband and wife suffer from ministry fatigue.
- It's a matter of spiritual warfare. Satan knows that any couple together in Christ is greater than the sum of its spiritual parts. He doesn't want them to ignite a spiritual flame, so he isolates them. He will do anything he can to keep the two of them from forming a spiritual bond.

Brian and I don't want to be one of those couples. We try to pray together every night, but we do struggle to be consistent. Jesus tells us that where two (or more) are gathered *in his name*, he is there. The key words are italicized. Your daily relationship needs to be powered by the authority of his name and the power of his presence. Pray together even when you don't feel like it. Cultivate a shared walk with Christ, and he will magnify your gifts so that you make each other stronger and better.

10. Make Your Spouse Your Project

We view each other as projects to constantly pursue and improve. A number of books have helped us do this. Tom Rath's *StrengthsFinder 2.0* gave us plenty to discuss together. We gained insights into each other's personal strengths and how we could complement them. *The Five Love Languages* by Gary Chapman is an eye-opening volume that looks at the way your spouse was created to love. Learning the special love language of your spouse can revitalize the way you show love.

A breakthrough moment for us came when Brian heard Wayne Cordeiro, senior pastor of New Hope Christian Fellowship in Honolulu, share some very valuable advice at a Willow Creek Leadership Summit a few years back. He spoke from his book *Leading on Empty*, and he addressed the benefits of knowing the things that fill us up and the things that drain us. When

Brian came home from the Summit, we went to Starbucks. We grabbed coffee and, on a napkin, we each wrote the things in our lives that were filling our tank and the things that we found to be draining. They're different for each person; what fills me may be the thing that drains you. We learned a lot about how to help fill each other up and how to be stopping agents for the drainers of life. And we've reworked the list several times, because it changes. We need to stay constant with each other, because we want to be on the same page.

Prayer, of course, heads the list of how we can apply ourselves to our "projects." Do you have a list of your spouse's prayer requests? I believe we're all running on empty at times, but we have the wonderful opportunity to help keep each other's tank full with the abounding love of God that never runs dry.

11. Set Meaningful Boundaries

Husbands, wives, listen very carefully: setting marriage above ministry requires careful boundaries. Marriage, ministry —which one does Satan want to destroy? *Both.* Look across the American church-scape, and you'll see how well he is doing in using one to undermine the other. We understand that we should be aware of him without fearing him. Our God is stronger, and our team has everything it needs to prevail. We just need to do what Brian's dad used to call "battening down the hatches." That means storm-proofing our marriages.

We've come to realize over the years that people come and go, and even staff come and go, and the only constants are God and the two of us; to lose us is to lose everything. Therefore we have set a few boundaries, and done so with care and sensitivity.

We talk about each other in public and onstage. We write about each other and our fun times together on blogs, Facebook, and Twitter. As I write, today happens to be Brian's birthday, and I was able to tell him on Facebook that he is the love of my life. People have the chance to see that our marriage is strong and happy. Those inappropriately attracted to one of us need not apply.

Brian doesn't ride in a car alone, or dine alone, with a woman other than family. He will not meet with female staff members unless the door is open. He doesn't counsel women; others do. If a woman must meet with him, he will ask his assistant or me to be included in the meeting. Ironically, Brian has been accused of "thinking he is all that" for setting these boundaries. On the contrary, wise leaders do these things because they know they're not "all that"; anyone can fall prey to temptation. He also wants to avoid anything that may appear inappropriate. Brian seeks every opportunity to deny Satan a foothold.

In our membership class at West Ridge, we make it clear that we can't be accessible to all people at all times, and we share that we will choose to value our family and spend most of our evenings together. Our church has simply grown too large for us to have dinners with even a small percentage of our members. People understand that, as long as we're clear with them about it. We find that they like to know our values, and they appreciate our spelling them out.

Social networking — one more medium for special care. Old flames pop up to "friend" us, and they recall the people we *used* to be. They can post all kinds of unwanted comments in a public place. A newspaper in the UK reported last year that Facebook has been cited in one out of five online divorce petitions. Here's our advice: never put anything in print — in a letter, email, text, tweet, or Facebook message — that you wouldn't want to see on the front page of the *New York Times*, where the whole world could read it. Because once you've put words into print, you don't know where they will end up.

Brian doesn't usually travel without another male staff member or friend. This is a policy set by the elders at West Ridge Church, and Brian appreciates it. The wide-open road is filled with temptations, and the stakes are too high. Again, we find the footholds for evil and try to eliminate them.

Never speak negatively about your spouse in front of others. It's amazing how many ministers will use their wives as the object of a joke or make implications about the tension in their marriage. By the same token, I've seen women gather to have a good male-bashing session, and I find these very unhealthy. Brian and I know

"How do you plant a church and also maintain a healthy marriage?" It is a great and challenging question. There were definitely times we weren't sure we had the answer. Like the very first launch team meeting when Sue heard Dave describe this new church that sounded nothing like the church we had come from, and she thought to herself, *This is not going to look good when I don't go to this church*. And there were the early years when Dave was pouring himself into the start of Community Christian Church and Sue was investing herself in a young family and it didn't feel like we were always playing on the same team. But now we are twenty years into this church plant; we love each other very much and are feeling like an unstoppable team. If you want to plant a church and maintain a healthy marriage, here is what we suggest:

1. Realize It Takes Teamwork to Make the Dream Work

As a couple, we share a passion for the mission of Jesus. It is that shared passion that has allowed us to make it through tough financial times, unjust criticism, and strained schedules. You definitely need to be on the same team if you want to plant a church and maintain a healthy marriage.

2. Play Your Position

Ignore the expectations and the roles that others have for you. Sue was never expected to play the piano or do children's minis-

that our marriage is a model that many other couples see, so hopefully you won't catch one of us throwing the other under the bus.

Even among our closest friends, our guards are never fully down. We recommend a higher level of openness with each other than with anyone else.

Finally, if your marriage is struggling, seek counseling. There is no dishonor in working with a good Christian therapist who

try just because she was the pastor's wife. We each understood our gifts and talents and played the position that God meant for us to play.

3. Don't Neglect the Farm System

We have often said to one another about our family, "If we blow it at home, we have blown it." So make your kids a priority. We made a lot of sacrifices for the mission, but we did not sacrifice our kids. Sue has always put being a mom ahead of church roles and has made family a priority. Dave has also made family a priority, which includes a weekly date with each of our kids. There are times you are going to have to disappoint someone; make sure it is not your kids.

4. Make Sure There Is an Off Season

One of the rhythms of our life is for the two of us to get away from the demands of church life. Sometimes it has been to fun and exotic places, and other times it was just a couple nights in Chicago. That time off for just the two of us gave us time to relax and reconnect.

— Dave and Sue Ferguson,
Community Christian Church, Chicago, IL;
Movement Leaders, Newthing Network

will respect your confidentiality. Just recently we spent time with a counselor for a tune-up. We've decided we're not satisfied with "good" or even "great"; we want the "best" for our marriage. Marriage is a supreme gift from God, and it can make or break your service to his kingdom. If you're serious about church planting, you can't do better than to heed the advice of Scripture:

> Two are better than one, because they have a good return for their labor: If either of them falls down, one can help the other up. But pity anyone who falls and has no one to help them up. Also, if two lie down together, they will keep warm. But how can one keep warm alone? Though one may be overpowered, two can defend themselves. A cord of three strands is not quickly broken.
>
> —ECCLESIASTES 4:9–12

If you are blessed to have a spouse, know that he or she is the greatest treasure God could give you, apart from the gift of his Son. Cherish that treasure. Nurture it. As time passes and people come and go, you'll discover that what remains is the two of you and God, the "third strand" from the passage above. Together there's nothing such a team cannot accomplish.

CHAPTER 5

HOW DO YOU PLANT A CHURCH WITHOUT LOSING YOUR FAMILY?

Upgrading Your Home Security System

Before Amy and I began working to plant West Ridge Church, we knew that our marriage would be a target for spiritual warfare. It was intuitive. For one thing, we were focused on being a team. Starting the church was a passion for the two of us together, so the two of us together would be tested. We were determined to reach thousands of lost people for Christ through a new church. There was no way Satan was going to simply leave us alone.

The most obvious way to derail our efforts, of course, was to create friction in our marriage. If the marriage falls apart, so does a couple's ministry. That's why we spent months solidifying our marriage when we moved to the Atlanta area. It wasn't that we weren't already solid; we definitely were. We simply wanted to be so tight, so much on the same page, that we would allow Satan no foothold whatsoever. So as tough as those times were for planting a church, they were good times for us as a couple.

We both came from ministry families that taught us a little about spiritual warfare but never put tremendous emphasis on it in the way that certain parts of the evangelical world do. We knew about Satan, who he is and how he tempts us; we just didn't see him behind every bush. We hadn't been forced to confront the idea of genuine demonic opposition at the level of everyday life. For us it was a little out there.

Still, we knew that starting a church would expose us more to spiritual conflict, and we did take the time and the initiative to safeguard our marriage. What we failed to consider was that Satan would come after our child. Yet why wouldn't he do that? We failed to think in those terms. Perhaps the thought of an attack on our son was just too frightening; children are so small, so fragile. Taylor was two years old. Aren't the terrible twos terrible enough, just naturally speaking, without having to cope with the supernatural?

Our deepest instinct as adults is to protect our little ones. Amy and I are fully committed to our vision of ministry, but if it were ever to become something that threatened our family, that negatively affected our children, we would walk away. We know that the highest responsibility God has given us is to care for each other, the next highest is to care for our two sons, and the next highest is to care for the church. So we work as hard as we can, from day to day, to keep all three healthy and in sync — marriage, parenting, and ministry. But it's easier said than done.

The truth is that Satan recognizes no boundaries or rules, other than the principle that he will flee when we resist him; it's our job to recognize when he is active and must be resisted. We need to realize that to him, everything in our lives and our families is fair game. Whatever he can exploit, he will. A friend of mine, Daniel Henderson, likes to say that Satan doesn't have to destroy you; he just has to distract you. What better way to distract you than to create turmoil in your family? And what better way to do that than to threaten your children?

Late one night, during the months just before our first church service, we had an experience that woke us from our naiveté about the spiritual security of a family. Amy recalls it well.

I (Amy) remember that we were still in the Lithia Springs apartment, and we were lying in bed in the middle of the night.

Suddenly we were awakened by a loud, horrifying noise, and we looked at each other: "What in the world is that?"

It sounded like a freight train in our apartment. We sat straight up in bed as we realized Taylor was screaming at the top of his lungs. Our apartment neighbors heard it too; they were pounding on the walls. But we were too frightened to worry about that. Taylor was standing at the end of our bed, with a look on his face that shocked us. He pointed a finger at Brian and said in a powerful voice, *"You are a bad man."* Then he pointed directly at me and said, *"You are a bad woman."*

I gasped, put my hand over my mouth. Brian immediately picked up Taylor; surely our son was walking and talking in his sleep — some kind of bad dream. Taylor balled up his fists and began punching his dad in the face as I sobbed and said, "No, Taylor!" It was an awful thing. Brian later said that these weren't the punches of a little boy; they were hard and serious blows.

We carried him back to his room and sat down on the end of his bed. Brian put Taylor on the floor in front of us; we didn't know what else to do. Brian began to pray: "In the name of Jesus Christ, you leave my son alone!"

We felt something like a wind around us, and Taylor fell forward like a wet noodle. He started to cry, and he was saying something like, "Will you help me?"

We were all crying. We carried him back to our room and put him in the bed with us. The three of us lay there and held each other. Taylor was scared on the level of a child who had awakened in the night, didn't know what had happened, but sensed something terrible. We were frightened too, but on a much deeper level.

Brian and I both understood exactly what was happening. We were thinking, *Satan, you come after us — but you stay away from our child!* Taylor wasn't even three years old. He was helpless, and we were coming to understand that we were at a stage of spiritual warfare we had never experienced before.

We became conscious of our need to watch over our children, not just in a physical or even emotional way but also in a distinctly spiritual way. And an attack wouldn't have to be as dramatic as that late-night experience; it could be something as simple as Satan trying to make our child believe a lie.

One day, when Taylor was seven, we gave him a big day. We bought him a new bicycle and took him to Chuck E. Cheese's. The day was all about having fun with Taylor. That night, when it was all over, we were putting him to bed. He said, "Nothing really good ever happens to me. I don't ever get anything good."

My first reaction was to be angry. How could he say that with a brand-new bicycle sitting in the garage and a whole day that centered on making him happy? But I thought about it for a minute and realized what was happening. Satan was lying to him. I sat down and said, "Taylor, think for a minute. Do you really believe that's true?"

I then reviewed the facts with him. We had a little talk about the lies Satan can tell us and how easy they are to believe. Taylor had a family that loved him, that was generous with him, but Satan wanted to keep him from being happy. We taught Taylor that Satan runs away when we worship God, talk about God's goodness, and focus on the truth. I said, "Let's try it. I'll say something and you say something. I'll start — God gave us a beautiful world."

Taylor said, "God loves me very much."

And I said, "He sent us his Son." And so on. We sang worship songs together and focused on God, and it became a memorable moment, a God moment.

Now our kids are older, and we help them understand that Satan lies to them on a different level and in more complicated ways. We make it a big point to educate them about spiritual warfare and help them understand how to recognize it and respond to it. Some will think it's a little weird to deal with these themes in a family. Maybe they're afraid of frightening their children. Brian and I believe that if you're doing something significant for God, you can't afford to be blind to this issue. We need to take seriously Ephesians 6:12, a verse that says that our struggle is not against flesh and blood; it's against forces from the heavenly realms.

Drawing the Boundary Lines

We struggle against those supernatural forces described in Ephesians, but we also struggle with "flesh and blood." We let down our families in purely natural ways.

Sometimes Satan doesn't have to lift a finger to oppose us, because he knows we have so many ways of getting it wrong on our own. In ministry and church planting, one of the greatest natural issues is that of boundaries. We discussed these in the previous chapter in regard to marriage. The stakes are also high when it comes to your children. They are younger and more fragile. We get only one chance to bring them up, and we can't afford to make too many mistakes.

I (Brian) can remember a time before I realized the importance of this. We've shared how Taylor spent his first two years in the midst of our student ministry. He was so accustomed to being around teenagers that he thought he was one himself. The students doted on him. Amy watched over him like a mother eagle and kept him within close reach. But he was as immersed in our ministry as we were.

As Taylor began to grow older, and as we came to Georgia to plant our church, the need for boundaries began to emerge. I didn't understand this very well for a while. I can remember a typical occasion when I was sitting on the floor, playing with Taylor. He was soaking up his dad's attention. Then the phone rang, and I got up to answer it. The call was about some kind of church issue, and it dragged on. I kept looking over to Taylor, who was watching me with those wide eyes. I could see the impatience— *When can we get back to playing, Dad?* But of course I stayed on the call; I wanted to put out whatever fire was burning.

I can no longer remember what that phone call was about. I'm sure it was something trivial in the great scheme of things. But far too well I can remember looking over to see that Taylor had left. He had given up and wandered away; Dad had something to do that was more important than him. That is the message I was sending him, whether I intended to or not: *Work is more important than you.*

When I finally realized I'd been doing this, I felt sick to my stomach. Every time I cut short my time with him to do something else, I was sending him that negative message. Of course, I didn't *feel* that he was less important; nothing in the world mattered more to me than my son. But what we feel is only one part of love. The other part is how we show it. What a tragedy when a spouse or a child or a friend has no idea how much they mean to us—or even get the idea that they don't mean much at all. I decided that if I was going to protect my marriage and my home, I was going to have to create hard and fast boundaries, then be consistent about observing them.

My boundaries begin with the realization that there is always ministry to do. There are always emails and phone calls to answer, church friends who need something, or someone in the hospital. As pastors or planters, we are shepherds at heart. We feel called to minister, and we also want people to know that we really care. Without boundaries, however, we will be consumed by the list of needs that is always growing. Our homes will always come in second place while we pursue the urgent things.

We all know this, of course. And yet Amy and I talk to many planters who seem to believe there's not much they can do about it. They've honestly never considered defining their boundaries and making them known. As we've shared our presentations on this subject, we've often seen their faces light up. It's as if someone has given them permission to do what God has always wanted them to do — care for their families. Outside of your relationship with God, your top priority is your marriage and your home. This is biblical; it's also common sense, and you should state it up front to your people without apology.

Boundaries at Home

Every leader must define his or her own boundaries. But perhaps it would be helpful for us to offer some examples of ours. We hope these will be an encouragement to you and an affirmation that it's possible to protect and nurture your family in the midst of a challenging ministry.

We don't answer the phone when we're having dinner. Family dinner is an important time for us to be together and share our day. A recent study of teenagers and their parents found that families that ate dinner together were far more likely to raise healthy and well-behaved teenagers. Also, the children from such families were more likely to report feeling a closeness to their parents. When you ignore the phone to listen to your child during dinner, you're showing your child who and what matters to you.

If I really need to return a call, I try to do it before I arrive home. If I pull into the driveway and I'm not finished, I will sit in the car until my calls are completed. I do my best to make my evenings belong to my family.

Call-screening is a valuable habit. I use voicemail and help from my assistant, then make decisions about what is truly important and what can wait until tomorrow. When I evaluate these matters objectively, I tend to see that most of them can wait until my office hours. Of course, there are occasional emergencies and special situations that must be attended to with urgency. Our kids understand that.

How about the computer? The Internet has a special magnetic power for us and can be one more obstacle to family time. We make it a point to limit our computer usage at home and engage with our family as much as possible. Social networking is a special category; too many church planters are working Twitter and Facebook even while sitting in their family rooms.

And then there's the cell phone. I can't tell you how often I have lunch with a friend who keeps looking at his phone, checking for texts and email and voicemail. Amy finds that the wives of planters are usually irritated and hurt by their husbands' constant need to be checking their phones. Are any of us really so important that we need to be networked every hour of the day? Don't take yourself so seriously; go play with your kids! When you're at home, as much as possible, put your phone out of the path of temptation.

As we began to start Genesis Church, we decided to be very intentional with how we valued our time and relationships as a family. From the beginning we put God first, each other second, our children third, and then whatever we might have left over, we give away to others. Although it is a constant battle, we fight hard to keep these values in place. Friday is our sabbath, simply meaning we cease. It's our day to intentionally stop working, rest, date, let God fill us back up, and remind ourselves that it's his church, not ours. God told the church in Revelation he would remove his lamp stand from them because they lost their first love. We decided to guard and keep our "first loves" in their correct order so that his lamp stand will continue to shine bright in the midst of us.

— Tim and Tandy Grandstaff,
Genesis Church, Orlando, FL

You may need to have it nearby for emergencies, but you don't need to check it incessantly.

Children and Expectations

Another area we must manage is the expectations that we — and others — place on our children. If we think about it, we realize there are more expectations for kids, in general, than ever before. It's a challenging world in which to raise children. But for the kids of church planters and leaders, we're talking about a whole different level. People look at them and see "pastor's child" as if it were stamped on their foreheads. Then they expect every word and deed from that child to match their conception of how a pastor's child should behave. One of Taylor's high school teachers even told the class to watch what they say because Taylor is a pastor's son. How embarrassing!

We can't often do much about that, of course. What we can do is prepare our children for it and make sure they know that we have no special or unrealistic expectations of them. It's not their job to be young public relations representatives for our church. If Taylor or Zach comes home and tells us that people are watching him and relating to him as a preacher's kid, we tell him to simply be himself, act appropriately, and beyond that, don't worry about what others think.

We know that pastors' kids are under the microscope too much, so we try to give our children permission to be themselves. As a matter of fact, when there are things they want to do, if we possibly can, we try to say yes. If it's something that's sinful, of course, we can't do that. But we try to let them experience the truth that living for Christ is a joyful, positive thing and not a list of don'ts. We set a high value on having a *normal* family life — in a healthy, loving, and enjoyable sense. We want church to be something our children want in their lives, rather than something required of them. So we don't set rules about their attendance. We don't have a "Christian music only" rule in our household.

So many church leadership families today are so worried about perception that they go the opposite way and load down wives and children with restrictions. That's a burden that children and spouses shouldn't have to bear, and it's the reason so many pastors are losing their families; it's one of the reasons why, according to George Barna, fifteen hundred of them per month are walking away from ministry.

Instead, we want our children to own their relationship to God, and to own it early in life. Taylor was seven years old before he understood that his dad was the *lead* pastor. He knew his dad was a pastor at West Ridge, but now his eyes were wide. He said, "You mean Dad's *in charge?*" That actually made us feel good, because it meant we hadn't built up the pressure about being in the pastor's family. We'd kept the church from consuming our home life.

Zach, our younger son, likes to say to Amy, "We don't care what people think, do we, Mom?" And we all laugh. That may be a funny way to put it, but he is reflecting the lesson he has learned from us: that if you live your life for God, you really don't have to worry about what other people think. That part will work itself out.

We tell church planters that we've come to use the word *appropriate*. What is appropriate? We ask our children to think in terms of godly principles and then try to do what is right for that time and place and situation. They shouldn't live their lives based on being the pastor's kid; they should live them based on the understanding that God loves them unconditionally. All of their significance, security, and acceptance can be found in Jesus.

We want our kids to love God with all their hearts. We want them to love people. And we want them to respect us as their parents.

In our house, Brian and I (Amy) want to raise leaders and world changers. We are very strategic about how we're approaching that goal, including which people we bring into their lives. However, we want our boys to leave our home with four truths deeply engrained in their minds:

- God loves you unconditionally (John 3:16; Eph. 3:19)
- You can trust him completely (Prov. 3:5 – 6)
- He will never leave you (Deut. 31:6; Heb. 13:5)
- Everything you need is "in Christ" (Col. 2:9 – 10)

If they can learn those two important truths, they're going to have a head start in growing to someday be the balanced, positive young adults we envision them being. We feel those would be terrific goals for any child, by the way. Their dad's being a pastor shouldn't change the way we raise them. Again, we want them to have a normal and happy childhood in a normal and happy home.

What about church activities? We let them decide the level of their involvement. Both of our boys are involved in sports, and they've played on traveling teams. There are many student events at church that they may end up missing. Baseball games may be scheduled for Sunday morning, so as a mother I sometimes choose to be at one of my sons' games instead of at our worship service.

We've known couples in ministry who might question that decision. They might argue that we must always hold up the example of church being more important than anything else. We believe God is more important than anything else. Jesus healed people on the Sabbath, and he spent most of his time with unchurched people. I would be deeply hurt if our boys grew to hate church because we wouldn't let them play baseball on an occasional Sunday. I think the answer here is to pray for wisdom and create a healthy balance.

At the same time, we want our children to be deeply involved in church for the same reason that their friends are: because they have chosen to be there. Brian has told our student pastor to expect this and not to view the attendance of our children as any kind of statement on his (Brian's) support for them or those events. Being pastor's kids doesn't mean that Taylor and Zach will participate in all church events. We ask our staff not to treat our boys any differently than any other teenagers in the church—no special privileges, no special attention. I think there are a lot of people in our church who don't even know who our boys are, and that's fine with us; Taylor and Zach don't need that fishbowl experience, just a normal, happy life in church, home, and community.

For the record, both our boys love to go to church. They attend the student worship service and summer camp and as many other activities as their schedules will allow. We're hoping they won't grow up feeling that church was an obligation and that this will allow them the full freedom to be themselves, guilt free. We try to create a family environment where our children can love God and love the church—and love is something that cannot be forced but must be given freely.

Building Children of Faith

Amy and I (Brian) grew up in homes in which we learned to trust God through hard times. Our families dealt with challenges —our dads were both in school and there was little money. We learned to trust God by seeing him meet basic needs. We would pray, and God would come through as we found that someone had placed money in the handle of our car door so that we could pay the electric bill.

Our question therefore was, how will our children develop a firsthand faith? The answer, we're learning, is that God allows different experiences in the lives of his people to move them toward total dependence on himself. Sometimes those experiences are painful and out of our control. It's a challenge for us, as parents, to stand back and simply let God work in the lives of our kids. There are times when we wish we could slap a few people, forget the big picture, and throw character building out the door on the way to rescuing our boys.

But we love our boys too much to deprive them of God's work in their lives. He wants to make himself known to them as helper, rescuer, provider, and promise keeper. It's our job to encourage, train, love, and support, but God has to become *their* God. He is the one who authored the manual of their lives and who plans to give them a hope and a future. We can't dictate that future, nor would we want to. But we can trust God to do his best work in their lives. On the other hand, we have learned that there are moments when we do have to step in and rescue our kids.

Zach had a teacher who singled him out in elementary school. We wanted to believe that it wasn't true, but the other kids were noticing. Their parents came to us about it. The teacher gave him a hard time nearly every day. Amy and I wondered what we should do. I'm embarrassed to admit that we were torn between our reputation as church leaders and the need to rescue our son. We wanted to maintain the most positive possible relationship with the school.

We delayed, and that was a mistake. The time came when we knew we had to talk to the teacher and raise the issue — but by that time it was too close to the end of the school year. We had worried more about our relationship with the community than about what was right for our son, and we deeply regretted it. From that day, we made the decision that we would never again sacrifice the well-being of our boys for the sake of ministry. No matter how you slice it, ministry children pay an occasional price for the homes in which they're raised. It's going to happen, but if there is significant harm threatening our kids, we need to do what's necessary to protect them. God has entrusted them to us — even above our ministries.

There are good moments too — teachable moments. We'll sit outdoors on our back deck in the fall, as the leaves change colors, and have a casual, unfocused family talk around our fire pit. The sun goes down, the breeze blows, and it's a wonderful atmosphere for togetherness. Soon our kids will find themselves opening up, sharing their thoughts, and we listen and take hold of whatever's on their mind, whatever issue is looming at that moment for them, to offer some little bit of wisdom they can use.

I heard someone say recently that parents today are so focused on giving their children everything they themselves never had that they forget to give them what they *did* have—the simple things in life, principles and values that were instilled in them as children, things that are far more valuable than the latest smartphone or video game. One of the things you can give your children is the firsthand experience of God's work. They can be on the front lines to see the changed lives of people or go on an overseas mission trip and see the mighty work of God. Each of our boys experienced their first mission trip to Jamaica at age seven and saw an entirely different world than the one they'd grown up in. Taylor just returned from a ten-day mission trip in the Dominican Republic, where two of his passions, God and baseball, came together. We want our children to see God with their own eyes rather than get the secondhand view that is filtered through our experience.

We've already said a few words about spiritual warfare. As church planters, you'll find that your children will experience things that none of their friends will have to live through, because Satan will always be trying to find a way into your home. At times there will be a kind of heaviness, as I call it—a kind of atmosphere you can't quite describe. It's so important to talk about these things with our children, making sure they understand the true issues. Spiritual warfare may feel like plain frustration, confusion, discouragement, depression, anger, hopelessness in the face of seemingly insurmountable challenges, or it may be the temptation to believe the lies that Satan tells. We want our children to know how to recognize spiritual warfare, to know it without fearing it; we trust in God and know Satan will flee if we face him with worship and praise of God and with the truth. When we or our children are tired, we tell them that this is just the time to expect temptations to pop up. Also, if God has just done or is about to do something incredible, we point out that this is just the time for Satan to try something. He looks for points of weakness, and he looks for points of spiritual progress that he can circumvent.

That all sounds very heavy, but we assure you that we spend the most time of all talking about the goodness and love of God. Every evening, we pray together as a family. When my boys go to bed, I go into their rooms, get close to their ears, and say three things: "God loves you. You can trust him. Because of Jesus, you've got what it takes." Then I tell them I love them.

Inevitably, I see a smile come across their faces, and they say, "Thanks, Dad. I love you too."

Planning as a Family

We talk with church planters about planning out a year. What we find is that they tend to plan their church year, then somehow fit their families' lives into that.

Instead, we tell them to "put in the big rocks first." Stephen Covey popularized this little illustration by taking out a wide-mouthed jar with rocks in it. He asked, "Is the jar full?" People said that it was. He said, "Not so fast," and then he poured in a handful of pebbles. "Now is it full?" he asked. The wary audience said that it probably wasn't. So he poured in some sand and seemed to fill it up. Full yet? No—he could still pour in some water. "What lesson did we just learn?" he asked.

"That you can always fit in something else," suggested someone.

"Wrong," said Covey. "The lesson is that if you don't put in the big rocks first, then you'll never get them in at all."

For us, the big rocks are our family. If we don't schedule time for our family up front, that time will never materialize. Amy and I schedule two getaways per year, just for the two of us. Then there are family vacations. These are scheduled before anything else is put on the church calendar. This is the right thing to do, and we have to get past people's criticism of it; we'll never please them all. Again, we care what God thinks, and we try to do what is appropriate.

Above all, perhaps, we make it a point to see our home as a safe place, a refuge from everything else. So many church planters and leaders feel that they're never off the clock and that their homes

We believe that if pastoral marriages and families are healthy (not perfect), church planting provides a great environment for families to become even better. Here are a few practical suggestions.

1. Your marriage should always take priority over your children and new church. There obviously must be balance, but children blossom and feel secure when they know their parents are crazy in love with each other and give their relationship top priority in the family. Our goal is to start each day by praying, "Lord, today help me to love Debbie (Tom) as Christ loves the church."

2. In church planting, the planter couple's home many times becomes the center of activity for the new church. Your office is in your home. Create healthy boundaries to protect your family so that your church work is not 24/7. When it is time for your marriage and family, give 100 percent attention.

3. Create family traditions. We have gone for at least two-week-long vacations for nearly thirty years, and we go to the same place, Lakeside, Ohio. Our kids knew that when it was Lakeside time, it was their time.

are simply extensions of the church office. It takes a good bit of discipline to keep the home as a place to get away.

We use the phrase "circling the wagons," referring to those old Western movies in which the settlers would form a circle with their wagons in order to watch each other's backs when they were surrounded by attackers. If one of our kids is having a tough time at school, or if there is criticism at church, we take care of one another at home, and we know we're safe there.

It's another reason why we've recognized that we can't invite everyone to dinner. We need to protect our family time and keep our home as a place where we can be completely ourselves and not be on the clock. In the long run, one of the greatest gifts you can give your children is a home where they feel totally safe, guilt free, and loved.

4. Make it clear from the pulpit that you are crazy in love with your spouse and children. This kind of modeling is good for the church and also says "stay away" to individuals and forces that might think about intruding.

5. It's important for dads to be home at night when the kids go to bed. There is something about bedtime that creates teachable moments that we don't want to miss.

6. Church planting is stressful. Don't paint a negative picture of the church. Church-planting families should be in love with the church. Let your children help out. If they feel like they are making a positive contribution as children, they will love the church as adults.

7. If your marriage or family has serious problems, *don't plant a church*! The new-church environment is no place to fix your family.

— Tom and Debbie Jones,
Stadia Church Planting Network

Everyone Needs a Rock

During my college years, there was a large rock in front of my (Brian's) parents' home in Michigan. During that period, it became a place for my dad and me to go when I was going through turmoil of any kind—a broken engagement, for example.

I went through most of the typical struggles that people must face on the threshold of adulthood. I was having my first experiences in ministry as a student pastor in New Jersey. Life was filled with questions and uncertainties. I would come home, begin to open up about my worries, and Dad would say, "Let's hit the rock." And we'd walk down the long gravel driveway, sit on that great boulder, and gaze at the stars as we talked about life and the hurts it could bring. Finally, Dad would lead the two of us in prayer, and by the time I climbed off that rock and headed indoors, I knew things were going to be all right.

Years later I had the joy of having my dad join our staff at West Ridge, where he continued to pour himself and his wisdom into the lives of younger men. Then came one of the most terrible days of my life. He had been away on a rafting trip with my adoptive brother, who was thirteen, when I received word that my dad had died in a tragic accident during the trip.

I stood before fifteen hundred people at his funeral, and I told the story of those times with my dad when he helped me to open up and to trust God. I told those people how I saw my dad as a rock in my life, someone who was always strong and sturdy for me. I told them how he had given so much of himself that I always knew I had someone to turn to—and how, like every good father, he had directed me toward the ultimate Father, the ultimate Rock, who loved us both.

I confessed that one of my dreams was to have a beautiful prayer garden adjacent to our church, one with a great rock like the one that had come to symbolize so much for my dad and me.

It would be a place where people could come when they were troubled or when they wanted to reconnect with God or simply pray and journal and bond with others.

Several months later I got a call from some friends at our church. "Pastor," they said, "you need to come up to church. We have something to show you."

I drove up, and I couldn't believe my eyes. Four good men who had been at the funeral had felt moved to get a flatbed truck, drive up to Michigan, call our cousin who had bought the house, and arrange to take possession of that seven-thousand-pound stone. They had brought it back to Georgia to resume its role in providing a setting for spiritual blessing.

So now if you drive down the parkway that connects our church to the highway, you can see that garden on the right-hand side. Tucked back into the Georgia greenery is my dad's rock. We receive cards and letters from people telling us about the great moments that continue to occur in that setting. "I sat with my grandson on that rock," read one, "and I led him to Christ."

I don't believe you need to go looking for boulders in your front yard to share in this kind of legacy. The true rock, you see, was within my dad; it was the rock who is Jesus Christ, who is strong and sturdy for all of us and who wants to help every parent bond with his or her children. Can you be that foundation stone for them? Will they be able to come to you throughout their lives, for wisdom and encouragement and the assurance that all will be well, as they learn to trust in God?

Make your family the rock that every child needs.

Questions to Think About

1. Does Your Life Show Evidence That You Truly Accept Your Marriage and Family as Your Most Important Ministries?

We all need to feel that we've been given permission to put our families first. There may be any number of factors that keep us from doing it: fear, pressure, or workaholism, for example. Every church planter needs to have a clear understanding of how challenging ministry can be for the members of his or her family. How are you caring for your loved ones at present? In what areas do you need to improve?

2. Have You Established Clear Boundaries So That You Have a Margin for Protecting Your Family?

These boundaries will not establish themselves. The good people of your church, well-meaning as they are, will not establish them for you. You'll need to be very intentional about making rules involving work hours, the telephone, the Internet, and other issues. Then you'll have to make certain that everyone knows and respects these limits. While you'll never make everyone happy, you'll be far more successful if you are clear in advance about your limited availability and why it is so important for the health of your family.

3. Have You Discussed with Your Family the Basics of Spiritual Warfare?

First, we leaders must be certain that we ourselves have no illusions about Satan's intentions for our ministry. We need to be completely convinced that spiritual warfare is real and deadly. We need to learn how to recognize it in all its many forms. Second, we need to educate our families, focusing on the ultimate good news that the one who lives within us is greater than the one who is in the world (1 John 4:4). Talk together about the goodness of God. Teach your children how to sing his praises so that they know they must be aware, but never fearful, of the challenge that spiritual warfare presents. Remind them that the best weapon against a lie is the truth, as Jesus showed when he was tempted in the wilderness.

4. Have You Developed a Strategy to Help Your Children Love God and Church?

Will attendance and involvement be a requirement or an option for your children? What will you do to prepare them for being the pastor's kids? How will you prepare other church staff to deal with your children? What can you do to keep your kids from burning out on church activities and spiritual life?

Amy and I know that we must prioritize to care for our personal faith, our marriage, and our children. Our lives and our ministries are built on this foundation. That's simply the way God has designed things. We've come a long way toward understanding that parenting is the greatest and hardest task we will ever face. We are the first to admit that we do not have it all together. Balancing family and ministry is a constant challenge, and we realize that at the end of the day, if our boys turn out well, it will be by the grace of God alone.

We pray that this chapter has helped you to think about your family, and God's desire for it, in new ways.

> Church planting has been a positive experience for our family, as we have had a renewed opportunity and "excuse" to reach out to our neighbors. Our kids love being involved in our church plant, because they are plugged into real life, using their own gifts. They are personally involved in hosting our small group, even passing out waters and popsicles at the park. We as a family are intentionally looking for new and creative ways to minister to those around us.
>
> — Ed and Donna Stetzer,
> Grace Church, Nashville, TN

CHAPTER 6

HOW DO YOU DEAL WITH GROWTH AND CHANGE?

When It's Time to Cross the River

When our younger son, Zach, was in elementary school, he brought home a science paper one day. Its title caught my (Brian's) eye: "Living Things Grow and Change." It was a lesson we'd been learning all too well: life is all about change, whether that life is biological or spiritual. There are times in life when that change is welcome — getting married, starting a family, leaving home to start college. There are other times when change can bring struggles.

During our first year at West Ridge Church, we struggled simply to stay alive. What a transition it was from the life we had enjoyed in Lynchburg, Virginia; we knew what God wanted, and we knew we would have to be tough. As I've already related, we were nearly out of money when a New Year's Eve phone call changed everything. A wonderful man from another church wrote us a check for thirty thousand dollars. Our staff wept together, knowing that God had come through for us miraculously. We were going to make it in January after all.

At about the same time, we received another significant check, this time for seven thousand dollars, from an organization that wanted to support us. We perceived that as God's vote of confidence in keeping our church alive.

It wasn't long after that when my friend Vernon Brewer,

president of the missions organization World Help, called and asked if he could send a group from Lynchburg to lead a special Sunday evening service for us. Normally we didn't meet on Sunday nights, but we were eager to listen as his group shared music and testimony about God's work in other nations.

The Sunday night came, and so did the World Help team, which had just returned from India. During the musical presentation, one of our members, Lei Ann Law, came to me and whispered, "I'm going to go get your wife. She needs to be in here." I told her that was fine, and after a few minutes Amy appeared and sat next to me.

"You Are Supposed to Be in There!"

During the early months of West Ridge Church, I (Amy) led the preschool area as a volunteer. In a church plant, you have to spread the workers you have to fill the jobs available. I was willing to help with the children, along with other volunteers, but I always felt it wasn't my permanent calling. I was missing out on the action, wanting to hear my husband speak and to be there when someone came to Christ.

At the time, Brian and I were praying for funding to hire a part-time preschool director, freeing me up to work more closely with Brian. But that night, during World Help's visit, I was busy assisting with the children beside my friend Christie Veale and my sister-in-law Dawn. At one point, one of my good friends, Lei Ann, came in and said, "Amy, I'll take over from here. You go into the service, sit with your husband, and let me watch the kids. You are supposed to be in there."

I smiled and said, "Lei Ann, that's so nice of you! But this is my job. I'll stay here."

She had an insistent look on her face. "No, you don't understand," she said. *"You are supposed to be in there!"* I wasn't certain why she was so adamant about this, but I was delighted to take her up on her offer. I thanked her again and made my way to a chair beside my husband. He gave me a smile.

The music came to a conclusion; then one of the team members began to speak. He offered this challenge: "For four thousand dollars, you can plant a church in India. Add in another five hundred dollars, and you can place a Bible in the hands of everyone in that community."

I had come into the room wondering why I was supposed to be there. It seemed clear to me now. I leaned over and whispered in Brian's ear.

Changes in Attitude, Changes in Gratitude

Amy provided the tipping point.

I (Brian) had been struggling as I heard the testimonies about the exciting things happening in Asia. God's Spirit was tugging at my heart, saying, *You've just been given thirty-seven thousand dollars. How will you handle that?* On the other hand, we had been desperate. How long were even these generous dollars going to last? The human tendency is to hang on for dear life, pinch pennies, make it last . . .

Then Amy, who usually was working in the preschool area, leaned over and said, "Brian, we need to plant a church in India."

It was just one of those moments that ended the wrestling, drove home to me so clearly what God wanted done. I huddled our leadership team together, and we all agreed. God wanted us to tithe on our new donations. And here was how: a new church in India. I rose and said, "God has blessed us. Now I believe he wants us to show our gratitude and our obedience." I explained that a tithe of our check, thirty-seven hundred dollars, would just about start a new church in India — and that if we passed the plate, we just might put a Bible in the hands of everyone in that village. I said, "I believe West Ridge Church is going to plant its first church tonight!"

You could feel the buzz in that elementary school cafeteria. It was unlike any offering time Amy or I had ever experienced. God was doing something, and everybody wanted to be part of that. When the plates came back, we had to count the money immediately, of course. The total came to the amount we needed, almost to the penny: eight hundred dollars to add to our thirty-seven hundred dollars, for the total of forty-five hundred dollars that would start one church and supply the right number of Bibles. Lei Ann had been right — God wanted Amy present to help me be bold enough to give something back to him.

I had cried when God provided that great check on New Year's Eve. Now our whole church was getting the opportunity to live and feel the miracle of God's providence. Things were different for us from that day on. Word got around: something was up at West Ridge Church! It piqued people's curiosity. Some of them even decided maybe we weren't a cult after all. The next Sunday, we had over two hundred people in attendance, and the momentum was almost tangible.

The moral of the story, of course, is that God blesses generosity. When we decide to be unselfish and reach out to grow his kingdom, he will "throw open the floodgates of heaven," according to Malachi 3:10, "and pour out so much blessing that there will not be room enough to store it." We felt overwhelmed with such an outpouring of blessing. Just as important, we knew our church had turned a critical corner. We had been tested and tried, and God had shown his faithfulness. When people see God's hand at work and know that church isn't just some Sunday game we play, a whole community can be galvanized.

Within a year we had three hundred people and decided to add another worship service. That brought more growth. We had to move to the gymnasium, even bringing in an industrial air-conditioning unit on a trailer each Sunday.

After three years in our elementary school, we had nine hundred people and graduated to the high school. This involved crossing the county line, and we lost two hundred people immediately; as we've said, some people feel county loyalty. But for the same reason, we picked up many more by moving. We had to supply air-conditioning, so we gifted our high school with a permanent air-conditioner at a cost of about seventy-five thousand dollars. We continued to grow, to the point where we were causing traffic issues in the area on Sunday morning.

By 2000 we knew our church would eventually graduate from the high school too. We were looking for land to build on and not finding it. Meanwhile, we were desperate for a preschool director. I remember the day I sat down and made God a list with fourteen requests on it. My faith was stronger than ever from seeing what God had done, so I was stepping out with a list of requests that would be impossible outside of God's intervention. Land for a new facility was on that list. So was a preschool director. I decided to fast for forty days as I lifted up these audacious prayers to God.

Show Me the Land!

I prayed my fourteen-point list every day and began marking off the requests one by one as God granted them. I sensed that this was another critical point in which God wanted to show himself mighty for West Ridge. Sometime during my forty days of fasting, I got a call from Jeff Chandler, a friend in College Park, Georgia, south of Atlanta. "We've heard about what God is doing at West Ridge. We have some money we need to give you. We don't even know why; we just know you should have it."

The contribution was just the amount we needed for hiring a preschool director. That was another big day for us.

But what about a new location? When would God come through on that one? The Noonday Baptist Association had told us it was going to give us a forty-two-acre patch of land right down the road. It was nearby, but it had some disadvantages: rocky soil, a creek, and so on. We were still eager to explore that option. Then, just like that, the donor died and the commitment was gone, though the association continued its dialogue with the family about the land.

I was praying, *Show me the land, Lord!* And I had a special place for that prayer. Every day of my forty-day fast, other than two rainy ones, I parked my truck on the land — the forty-two acres we had been promised. For some reason, that's where I wanted to pray; I just felt drawn to that land, even though it didn't seem to be our future home. There was a great boulder there, tucked down into the woods. I took my list there every day and put my requests before God.

God answered my prayers miraculously, one at a time, until I had marked thirteen items off my list. Only one was left. I kept asking God to show me the land. I knew it wasn't quite time for us to build, but I wanted to know a general location that God had for us. On the final day of my fast, I received a phone call from the director of the Noonday Association. He seemed to call me out of the blue; we hadn't talked in some time. He said, "Brian, I'm sorry. We just can't get that land for you." I understood, and I knew it just meant that God had something else in mind for us.

Months went by — about thirty-six of them, actually — and we continued to grow. Soon, we knew, we would *have* to find a place to build. It was now 2003, and we already knew that the once-promised acreage wouldn't have been sufficient. One day, the Noonday director called and asked me to meet him at the property. Amy and I both felt it was probably a waste of time, because we had outgrown that acreage. But the director was still patiently working on strategies for us to get the land and build on it.

As I was showing him my favorite rock and other sites, my phone rang. It was Scott Laughridge, a member of our church who was a real estate developer. "I believe I've just found the property for our church," he said. "An elderly woman has died, and her adult children want to sell the acreage she owned." I asked for more details, and he said, "Stand by," and hung up.

Then he called again. "Where are you?" he asked.

"I'm about half a mile south of East Paulding Drive on Highway 92."

"What side of the road? East or west?"

"West."

"Brian, the property is across the street from the spot where you're standing."

Soon his car pulled up, and we looked at the wonderful acreage God had set aside for us. I was laughing, and for this reason: I'd had a list of fourteen prayer requests and believed I had thirteen yeses and one no. That no was for "Show me the land." Each day, three years earlier, I'd said that to God, then hopped off my rock and walked north on Highway 92. For thirty-eight days of a forty-day fast, I had been looking at what would eventually become the main entrance to West Ridge Church. It was sixty acres of beautiful land. I just didn't know what I was seeing.

Fourteen yeses after all. Just how great is our God?

The woman who had owned the land had been a wonderful Christian, and her children honored her request that her land always be used to bring honor to God. They sold us the land at about one-third the going rate, even with offers from commercial developers. Word continued to circulate in our community: God was doing something special at West Ridge Church.

Seasons and Reasons

As church planters, we live very much in the now. We have moments of envisioning a great, rosy future, but there is so much immediacy and urgency about our work that we deal mostly with the present. Most of the time, if God gave us a window into the future, we would be shocked by the things he has in store, so unpredictable to us.

It's important to realize from the very beginning that the church is a living organism, something ever changing. Churches grow and shrink and adapt and evolve just as human beings do. There are seasons in a church's life — sometimes planting, sometimes harvesting, sometimes clearing the wreckage of storms. As the poetry of Ecclesiastes 3 reminds us, "There is a time for everything, and a season for every activity under the heavens" (v. 1).

You've seen so far that we had times to weep and times to laugh in the early days of West Ridge Church. It's part of the growth process, not only for a church but also for the people whom God is using to build it. There is a kind of rhythm to church life, and as the years go by and you observe how God does things, you can pick up on it. There comes a critical moment when you sense God is bringing things to a halt and asking you, *Are you ready to go with me to this next level?* It's a season of testing.

The children of Israel had a river to cross. They came to a river and knew that God had reserved a place for them on the other side. This was their moment to answer the question. Were they ready to cross the river and go on to the next level? It involved a beautiful land of milk and honey.

Churches come to those rivers of decision all the time. It takes courage to cross over and face the "giants," the great obstacles perceived on the other side. *Does our church have the money? Are we really ready? What if something bad happens? Pastor, maybe we're already as big a church as we need to be.* Church is change,

change is challenge, and there are always people who don't particularly want any such disruption in their lives. They want quiet Sundays with a few extra activities, and they think their church should be the same yesterday, today, and forever — though that Bible verse refers to *Jesus*, not the church. These people ask, "Why can't things just stay the way they are?" But the only life that never changes is God; all other life, once it ceases to move onward, dies.

Pastors are familiar with "growth markers," round numbers that serve as milestones of growth. Crossing one hundred in attendance is a moment to celebrate; then two hundred, then five hundred, and so on. But with each milestone, your church is just a little different, just a little new. And some don't like that at all. Every pastor hears the whispers, "I think we're getting too big, if you ask me." Some of these members will eventually leave, which is a reasonable decision for them. There are people who are going to be happier in small churches, others in medium-size, and so forth.

It's not all about numbers, of course. God takes churches to new levels of maturity and faith too. God could test your church financially, as he did with us. Will you pass the test of generosity? He could test you through opportunity. Will you honor him in missions and in support of other ministries?

But people often respond most to the size issue. I can remember that when we first moved to Georgia, Amy and I believed that God would give us huge numbers of people right away. But he knew we couldn't handle it. God loves us enough to give us only what we *can* handle, *when* we can handle it. Then he says, *If I'm going to trust you with more, you'll need to make some changes and adjustments. Now, are you ready to cross the river?*

Growing Pains

There was a time when Brian and I (Amy) knew we were experiencing growing pains. It was wonderful to see our church grow, to see people coming to Christ every week. But we had new issues we'd never considered.

One day we were in our truck, in the parking lot adjacent to Sam's Wholesale Club in our little town of Hiram. We were talking about those painful moments when we couldn't remember someone's name. Brian has an amazing memory and has always prided himself on remembering names, and even at times people's telephone numbers. In the early days of West Ridge, when the church was smaller, remembering names was no problem. But now, with our rapid growth, things were different.

We would run into people in a restaurant and meet them for the second or third time, and they'd say, "Hi, Brian! Hi, Amy!" We would smile politely and greet them as warmly as we could. But we'd gotten to the point where we just couldn't keep all those names in our heads. The big issue, particularly for Brian, was the appearance of not caring enough about people to know who they were. That was something that mattered deeply to both of us. Brian agonized over the idea that anyone would think he saw himself as some kind of rock star who didn't care about anyone in his church. We were the same people we'd always been; it was the church that had changed! It was much larger. How could we let people know we cared if we couldn't even recognize them?

Sitting in our truck in the Sam's parking lot, we had a conversation that marked a pivotal point in our leadership. I could see that Brian was wrestling with this new issue; he couldn't tolerate the idea that people would misunderstand him. He simply hadn't had to face something like that in the past on such a scale.

The two of us deeply believed in reaching unchurched people for Christ. To do that, and to do it effectively, will always bring growth. It will bring this same problem. Brian and I realized that pastoring limited numbers and having everyone understand him all the time (as if that were possible anyway) was ultimately not God's plan. Instead, he needed to become mentally tougher, be as loving as possible but accept that he was going to be misunderstood.

We decided together that we would unapologetically grow and change with our church. We would press on in the direction in which God was clearly moving, even at the cost of being misunderstood. All we could do was to be as humble and loving to people as we could and help them understand that a growing church brought challenges. Brian needed to understand that he couldn't remember every name, and the members of our church needed to understand that he still loved them but could never be all things to all people.

Jesus was perfect, and he was still misunderstood. We couldn't expect any less. We knew that even after we explained what we had learned and decided, still there would be some who would not or could not understand. Some of them had gone as far as they could go with us. A few would accuse us of being aloof and power hungry. They would claim that all we cared about was big buildings and numbers.

> When we made the multisite transition, I (Pete) realized that I felt like I was such a loving person that I wanted to do everything for everyone, but I realized that really it was because I was wanting to *be* loved. My desire to be loved was growing faster than my desire to be loving, and so I was still trying to do everything — all the weddings, baptisms, counseling people. I was trying to fight the idea that I was inaccessible or that as the church had grown, I had changed. My desire to be loved was destroying my ability to be loving. The most loving thing I could do for those people was to let someone else help pastor them. Our elders helped us walk through this transition. It was hard to let go of those things, but now I am so much healthier.
>
> — Pete and Brandi Wilson,
> Cross Point Church, Nashville, TN

We weren't crazy about that, but we understood that it came with the territory. We weren't supposed to build our lives around what people think or say. There was only one audience whose opinion ultimately mattered, and he wanted us to keep reaching people, to embrace growth and change. He had given his life so we could do that, and he would be all that we needed.

Crossing the River

Amy and I (Brian) understood that we had come to a river-crossing moment. I had to decide how to respond and whether I could go to the next level with God — a church continuing to grow and take on more and more people. I believe God brings people and churches to these moments all the time, and there is always something wonderful to be gained, and some kind of baggage that must be left behind if we are to reach that farther shore.

For me, the baggage was the idea of pastoring a large church while continuing to micromanage the perception of me that hundreds of people had. If our church was going to go to the next level, I had to grow. And, in many ways, our people did too. It helped to be open with the church about this. One Sunday morning, during what we call a "family moment," I came to the front of the stage, sat on a stool, and spoke from my heart. "I need to be honest with all of you about something I've been dealing with," I said. I talked with them about the growth of our church, about how I felt whenever I couldn't recall a name. "You have to know that I love you but that my mind and memory have limits," I said. "I've agonized over it, but God has continued to grow our church. This means that some of you won't feel as close to us personally as you have in the past. It's hard for us, because we love you. And some of you will feel called to leave, because you'll decide it's a high priority for you to have a pastor who knows your name. Amy and I understand that. But we're at a crossroads as a church. We just need to be up front about where we are and where we're going." People respond well to honesty. A few of them left, with our blessings, and we moved on.

We still hear those whispers, "West Ridge has *changed*," when something happens that people don't like. It's just part of leading a growing church. If you can tell a tree's age by counting its rings, maybe you can tell a church leader's age by counting the layers of his skin. It has to get thicker and thicker.

This position isn't for the overly sensitive.

Laser Focus

Not long before Dr. Falwell died, I visited him and we had lunch at a little hot dog place he liked. I said, "Dr. Falwell, you're probably the most criticized person in ministry that I know — starting your own church, starting a university, a national movement, a seminary, becoming a national figure. How do you deal with the criticism?"

He said two words: "I don't." He smiled, took a bite of his meal, and said, "If I took on every critic who came after me, I would never accomplish the mission that God has given me to fulfill."

He was absolutely right. I remembered the story of Nehemiah traveling back to the ruins of Jerusalem to rebuild the walls. As he worked with his men, he stood on the ladder with a hammer in one hand and a sword in the other. His political neighbors tried everything they knew to distract him — criticism, requests for meeting after meeting. Nehemiah sent the same message each time:

> "I am carrying on a great project and cannot go down. Why should the work stop while I leave it and go down to you?" Four times they sent me the same message, and each time I gave them the same answer.
>
> —NEHEMIAH 6:3–4

One of your tests as a church planter will be to keep the work going even when distractions of every kind come. You need to realize the true source of distractions, the true enemy who wants to keep you from building. No less than Nehemiah, you are carrying on a great project. You can't afford diversions and distractions.

This is why you'll need to become very comfortable with the word *no*. Hold fast to your church's vision and mission, and when people come to you with some program idea that seems like a tangent from your main direction, measure their request against the great purpose for which God called you to lead. Remind them what the mission is.

Sure, you could take the path of least resistance and give in to pressure. But you'll be sorry later. Churches can become bloated repositories of little program-kingdoms people have built for themselves, and each one is costly. Each one diverts your people—in attention, energy, and resources—from the task you are called by God to carry out. At West Ridge, we subscribe to the belief that not every church is called to do every ministry. We are willing to admit we do some things well, but not all things. If we can't achieve something with excellence, we'll give it a pass.

Amy once attended baby showers for every new mother in the church. We hosted bridal showers and baby showers for church members. There comes a time when a church is too large to be able to do that. Does it mean we've gotten too big to care? Not at all —just that we are using different tools and strategies to care. We urge planters to think about every precedent they set. For example, the pastor might enjoy calling every church attender on his or her birthday. What happens on the first day when he can no longer do that, because there are so many names and he'd be on the phone all day? The first attender left out will be very hurt. So we really need to plan for growth and change from the very beginning.

As we've said, you must develop a little toughness, even be "mean" about your vision at times, as my friend Shawn Lovejoy says. Jesus must have seemed a little ill-tempered to Peter when the disciple tried to divert him from the road to the cross. " 'Get behind me, Satan!' he said. 'You do not have in mind the concerns of God, but merely human concerns' " (Mark 8:33).

I'm not recommending that you refer to any of your members as Satan. The point is that it often takes uncommon discipline to move toward your goals. You need laser focus, often in the form of that powerful, two-letter word *no*.

> When Martha and I started C3 Church over thirteen years ago, we had no idea the stress and challenges that would come along with it. But from the beginning we determined we would hold on to each other and stay focused on the vision that God had given to us. What has helped us is keeping our marriage a priority and having a weekly date night. Even in the crazy seasons of church life and growth, our times together remind us of what is really important in life. And as we lead the church, we stay focused on why we are doing what we are doing. It's not about us … it's about Jesus and what he has called us to do as we reach out to hurting people. Leading a church through changes and growth isn't easy, but it is so worth it when you see the lives of people change and the hurting find hope in Jesus.
>
> — Matt and Martha Fry,
> C3 Church, Clayton, NC

Ages and Stages

Churches and their leaders both move through seasons of life. It's important to have a good idea of where you are, as well as where your congregation is, on the timeline. Pete Richardson of the Thomas G. Paterson Center pointed me to insights from the ancient Hebrew understanding of the six stages of a man's life, also shared in Robert Hicks's book *The Masculine Journey: Understanding the Six Stages of Manhood.** These are very general, of course; the ages aren't precise, and the journey is a bit different for everyone. The main point is that our focus changes as we move through these seasons, and though we may engage in several of the basic tasks at a particular stage, there is usually a central issue in each one.

Each life stage is associated with a Hebrew name, as follows.

Birth – 12: Adam — The Creational Male. Childhood is simply the time for laying the foundation of manhood.

Ages 13 – 29: Zakar — The Sexual Male. A central issue in the twenties, of course, is finding a mate and then beginning a family. Therefore, at this stage sexuality emerges as the central issue of expression.

Ages 30 – 39: Gibbor — The Warrior. Having built the home base, the male turns to strengthening and defending it. This is, in modern life, the issue of career building that is often central to men in their thirties.

Ages 40 – 49: Ish — The Wounded Warrior. The warrior returns with battle scars. In modern work life, there will be disappointments and setbacks. The great issue is how do we deal with them? At this stage men often realize they're not as far along as they expected. You could call it midlife crisis. At this point men reassess their remaining years.

Ages 50 – 59: Enosh — The Spiritual Mentor. At about fifty, the male has a realization: "I have had some experiences and accumulated some wisdom." He begins to seek out younger men and finds satisfaction in helping to guide them along. The fathering side of him takes center stage as he begins thinking less of success and more of significance.

Ages 60 and Beyond: Zohen — The Patriarch. The mellowing

---

*Colorado Springs: NavPress, 1993.

years are heavily invested in the lives of others. The male finds himself at the center of a little world that craves the wisdom of his experience. He realizes that with all the blessings and the curses he has experienced, God has given him something to say, and he speaks back across the cycle to those at its earlier stages.

We need to see ourselves as works in progress, as people who are changing and developing, and we need to see the people around us in the same way. What is most important to a twenty-five-year-old? How can we better address those issues in our church? What about our patriarchs? How can we give them a better forum that honors the wisdom gained from all they've experienced?

The Big Takeaway

The year 2003, when God gave us our land, was one of those significant moments for our church. That summer, the elders decided to offer me a sabbatical. I appreciated their gesture and told them I wanted to use my time to attend a pastors' conference. The only one available during that summer, as it turned out, was a conference for worship pastors at Saddleback Church in Southern California. I wasn't sure it would really touch on my needs, but I decided to go anyway. I enjoyed the seminars and sessions, hearing from a variety of inspiring church leaders. Now there are conferences going on all the time, but at this time this was the only one offered.

My prayer was that I might take away something special from the experience. If I'm going to fly across the country, I want it to be a good investment of my time and the church's funding. I wanted to hear from God about the next level, about where we should be aiming with our ministry. Each morning of the conference, I renewed my request to God for a good takeaway.

It was a four-day event, and on the final morning, I woke up with an idea of going to the beach with my Bible and my journal; maybe God wanted to speak to me in a quiet place rather than among four thousand worship leaders. Sitting by myself on a beach is my idea of heaven, and journaling is the way I organize my mind and spirit and keep them grounded in what God is doing.

Then again, Rick Warren and Max Lucado were speaking during the final sessions. How could I miss that? So I went back and forth, and it just seemed like that little voice inside me was saying I needed to go and hear from these great communicators —even as I felt the beach calling too. At the first presentation that morning, Rick Warren unveiled the principles that would become his classic book *The Purpose Driven Life*. I listened intently; it was clear that he was onto something important.

There was a break, and I was thinking, *I'm glad I heard that. Maybe now I can go to the beach*. But the same little voice that had gotten me there that morning said, *Stay*. So I stayed, and Max Lucado came to the podium. Lucado said, "Well, I'm in a little bit of a predicament here. I'm here as Rick Warren's guest, and I just heard his great talk, but I feel that the talk I prepared for you might contradict *his* in certain ways." *Okay*, I thought. *This sounds interesting*.

He went on to describe how he'd asked an elder mentor of his to think over his life and share the greatest thing he'd ever learned. The man had said that it was this: "It's not about me, it's not about you, and it's not about now. It's about the glory of God." And there I had it: the moment I had asked God to give me, the takeaway that would refresh my ministry at West Ridge. The concept was so simple and yet so breathtakingly different from the way we live on an everyday basis.

We live and think and act as if the universe revolves around us, but none of it makes sense unless we understand the truth—it's *all* about God and his glory. We become consumed by our goals, by *our* this, by *our* that, while we're all just components of an incredible destiny that he is carrying out, of which we can see only the smallest corner.

The message swept over me, laid me out spiritually, and apparently it did the same for Rick Warren. He came up at the end and said, "Now I need to rewrite the first chapter of my book!" He did a great job pulling together the two central messages, which of course didn't conflict at all when all things were considered.

He did rewrite his first chapter. The first words of *The Purpose Driven Life* are, "It's not about you." Lucado himself went on to write a book called *It's Not about Me*.

As for me, I went to the beach after all, with my tall, skinny vanilla latte from Starbucks. At beautiful Laguna Beach, I sat and rewrote the purpose statement of my life, and I had my takeaway: "It's not about me."

Immediately God showed me an opportunity to begin bringing together other churches in the Atlanta area for community transformation. We started Engage Atlanta with the purpose of encouraging churches to work together to engage our community with the love of Jesus Christ. This past July we saw 110 churches come together to accomplish one thousand projects. We also started, in 2005, the West Ridge School of Church Planting. We have been able to train over sixty-five church planters and launch over fifty churches in the United States, and fourteen internationally. During 2010, God led us to start the LAUNCH Church Planting Network, and during this past year we established five training centers across the United States, trained twenty-two new church planters, and started eight new churches.

We were already on our way to building a growing church, but we wanted to be about more than that. We wanted to unite other leaders and congregations to say, "It's not about us and our walls and our ministries; it's all about building God's kingdom. We are all part of this thing God is doing, and we're cooperating to glorify him and carry out his purposes." We wanted to be a multiplying church. We wanted to change the scorecard we used to evaluate success. It wasn't just about being "attractional." God had now led us to be strategically missional.

I thought back on Max Lucado's great line, "God doesn't exist to make much of you; he exists to make much of himself." I knew I wasn't guilty of building a big ego kingdom to glorify my name at West Ridge. But now I really grasped how small our usual concerns and goals are in the great scheme of what God is doing. And I knew how much sense it makes to organize ourselves around *making much of him*. It was another river-crossing moment for our church and for me. This is the life of growth and change, as God brings his people along on the journey of a lifetime. You start out with the best of intentions, and God continues to pull back the curtain and show you a greater, more breathtaking picture. It's like starting to see a pebble, then seeing the gulley it's in, then eventually seeing the Grand Canyon. You could never have imagined how glorious the great vista of his work is.

Be ready for growth. It can be uncomfortable, it can be painful, but it can also be downright exciting. Yet God is taking *you* on a journey too. And when you get a glimpse of where he's taking you, you'll never want to look back.

Questions to Think About

1. Do You Have a Thorough Understanding of This Stage of Your Life and the Stages That Preceded It?

As we've seen, the seasons are often the reasons for why we behave the way we do and why we seek certain things. Have you identified the key issues of the stages in your life? What great issue is most critical to you right now, and what effect will it have on your efforts in church planting? What about your spouse? Your children?

We've seen that the struggle to plant a church will expose weaknesses and magnify personal flaws for everyone to see. You don't need to be perfect to pursue this future, but you do need to have a good bit of self-understanding. And as much as you do understand about yourself, be sure that you're about to learn a good deal more.

2. Are You Courageous Enough to Embrace River-Crossing Moments?

We've talked about river-crossing moments—times when God brings life to a halt and asks us if we are willing to go on with him to the other side or to the next level. These are faith-building moments, and they involve uncertainty and high risk. At the outset of each river-crossing moment in the life of a church, you as the leader will need to set the tone in handling them. How have you dealt with crises in the past? Have you embraced risk and change, or have you tended to back off?

3. How Thick Is Your Skin? Can You Handle the Criticism That Comes with Growth and Change?

No matter how prepared you are for growth moments, you can count on having any number of people around you who won't understand. When the Israelites first sent spies into the Promised Land, only Joshua and Caleb could clearly see what God's desire was for his people; the others in the scouting party gave in to fear and doubt. Can you handle the prospect of people whispering about your leadership, saying you are too ambitious, too egotistical, too impractical, and that your teaching is too shallow? Can you handle being misunderstood? How will you handle your critics?

4. Can You Be So Stubbornly Focused on Your Church's Mission That You Can Say No to People Who Lobby for Unnecessary Ministries and Programs?

A great number of people pleasers end up in ministry. They worry about how they are perceived, and they live to raise their approval ratings. Graciously, gracefully saying no is both an art and a discipline. But it will be essential to articulate your church's vision and why it's so important not to let your church become weighed down with competing agendas and unnecessary expenditures of energy, time, and resources.

A related question: Can you handle people walking away? You may decide, for example, that your church needs to discontinue a popular program that is no longer effective. What if a large group of people threaten to leave the church? Will you stand firm, or will you compromise the mission of the church?

5. Can You Personally Delegate Rather Than Micromanage?

Micromanagers often thrive in young and small churches, in which they can have a hand in everything that goes on. They may struggle to adjust to a growing church that forces them to delegate responsibilities. As your church changes — in this way or some other — you will be challenged to grow and become a different kind of leader. Do you understand your current leadership style? Do you believe you're capable of adapting that style to a fluid situation and a future filled with twists and turns that only God anticipates?

We don't want to give the idea that a leader must become something that goes against his or her natural gift set. Andy Stanley has said, "Don't try to strengthen your weaknesses; work on building your strengths." Then the strategy is to find other people to do what you cannot.

Still, growth in your church will require growth in you. This is the time to foster constant personal development and seek the wisdom of mentors. Will you embrace that kind of growth?

CHAPTER 7

HOW DO YOU BUILD AND LEAD A STAFF?

The Care and Feeding of a Dream Team

It's always darkest before the dawn. It was November of 1997, and we were still several weeks away from that wonderful New Year's Eve when God showed up for us in such a remarkable way. In the weeks before Thanksgiving, things seemed very dark for us. As a matter of fact, our situation was as desperate as it could be. I've described the financial crisis we were facing and the sagging attendance that was so discouraging to us after the months we had invested in starting West Ridge the right way. But the worst of it all may have been the criticism that seemed to be coming from the outside and the inside.

There was external criticism. There had never been a church like West Ridge in our community. We represented a threat to all the conventional ideas of how a church was supposed to be operated, because of our music, our casual style, even our location. The last thing on our mind was any desire to lure people away from the churches they were already attending. We were targeting the people who weren't going to church at all, and we wanted to lead unbelievers to Christ. If anything, we wanted to partner with the existing churches, not compete with them. But of course they didn't always see it that way, so there was a lot of negative talk.

More difficult still was the criticism that was internal. Many people who were attending West Ridge had their own ideas about what we needed to do, which programs we needed to start, and who should lead those programs. Sometimes it had to do with the student ministry, sometimes the children's ministry, most often music or worship issues. These were good people, but they had strong ideas and they saw our start-up church as a place for them to promote those ideas.

They came to me and argued their points. If they didn't make progress, they went to another staff member or to a staffer's wife. It was very frustrating for us. There was so much work to be done, but we couldn't seem to get much traction while dealing with all of these competing and conflicting agendas.

Finally the crisis came to a head. One evening during that November, Steve and Christie from our planting team hosted the other three staff members and their wives in their living room for a serious time of prayer and discussion. When I say serious, I mean that disbanding the church was on the table. If our team couldn't handle this criticism, we contended, then there was no point in going forward. Something had to give, because we would never break through and become a healthy, growing congregation while the atmosphere was so disruptive. *Unity is essential for any church.*

As we well knew, attendance was going down anyway; finances were dwindling. Science teaches that a living creature's response to acute stress is fight or flight. You engage or back away. Our team of four and our families had a choice before us. We tried to see our situation as God saw it. We knew he wanted us to succeed; he had called us here for a reason. So we looked around at the little group of eight and asked, "Where is the attack coming from?" What was the point where we were taking the most damage?

We figured it out. It was one specific ministry, one staff member who was the recipient of the most hurtful criticism. It wasn't that he was doing anything wrong—just that he was catching the most flack. So now we had a more specific understanding of our situation, and we had a decision to make: fight or flight?

No, that wasn't it; the better description was *faith or fear.*

To give in to fear was to say either that we didn't trust God or that we had been wrong about where he had called us. To respond in faith meant that we had heard his calling clearly, and we would claim his promises to uphold us and empower us. We chose faith. We decided to lock arms as a staff. The ancient Spartans used large, well-made shields that had hooks on the sides. They could march forward, side by side, with those shields locked together to create a solid, nearly impenetrable front. They were very hard to fight because they were so interconnected.

That was what we'd have to do. It would mean having each other's backs, refusing to listen to anyone who came to us to criticize another staff member. It would mean working together to strengthen the place that was taking the greatest part of the attack. As long as we held together and supported each other, we would be greater than the sum of our parts. Satan always seeks to divide and conquer, so locking shields was the right idea for us.

We decided to have one strategy for external criticism and another for internal. We would refuse to engage the external criticism. It wasn't our role to take on the world; we would have to take the Nehemiah approach there—building the walls and refusing to be distracted by outside forces.

Internal criticism, however, was different. These were our people, this was within our walls, and the worst thing we could do was to turn a deaf ear to it. Instead, we would take the initiative, confront the criticism, and deal with it openly. We believe this is an important principle. As we talk to church planters today, we find that many of them are nonconfrontational when it comes to internal criticism. They believe that "this too shall pass" or that the problems will fix themselves. What happens is that the criticism gathers momentum, like a snowball rolling downhill. Little issues can lead to huge church problems when they're not handled early.

This doesn't mean we attack our critics in the world's way, with claws out. We face them honestly, lovingly, graciously, using biblical principles of conflict resolution. Sometimes problems can be solved simply by mending relationships, building bonds with people whose true agenda represents some other, deeper hurt. "A gentle answer turns away wrath, but a harsh word stirs up anger" (Prov. 15:1). Other times, we need to affirm people in their need to go somewhere else, with our blessings. As Andy Stanley has said, "For what's at stake, you must do whatever it takes."

What was at stake in our crisis was the work God wanted to do in northwest Atlanta. We decided that his plans were worth whatever challenges lay ahead for us. So at the crossroads of fear and faith, we chose faith. In Steve and Christie's living room, we got on our knees and prayed together, rededicating ourselves to West Ridge, to God, and to each other.

Within a few weeks, our financial crisis had been resolved. Then when we tithed our gift to plant the church in India, our attendance turned around. There was such a groundswell of spiritual anticipation that a certain amount of the criticism dwindled away. Once again we had learned that the faith response leads to higher ground—a new level of service to God. Not that the criticism ever goes away for good. No matter how you grow, how much success your church has, how well you serve God, there will be critics. Sometimes the criticism is the worst for the very reason that you're being obedient to God. Spiritual warfare is simply the sign that you and God are at work together.

So be prepared. When you plant a church, you and your team will need to lock shields, as we decided to do. Building and nurturing a church staff is one of the great blessings and challenges of ministry.

Team in Transition

I'm constantly asked about building and leading a staff. Church planters are anxious about this particular issue, and it's easy to understand why. As pastors, we pour a large portion of our time into the team we've put together. We meet with the staff, we deal with staff issues, and we consult the staff for help on specific problems that arise. We need a strong team, because ministry is challenging, and a chain is only as strong as its weakest link.

You learn that truth quickly enough when you plant a church. Your own calling, in the beginning, is a matter between you and God. Then, in time, you need to bond with a team to move forward toward that vision. But when a staff develops issues, you can become entangled in ways that will undermine all you seek to accomplish. The team must constantly be rebuilt and replenished. Just as people in your church will come and go, so will people on your staff. Sometimes when team members are highly effective, they'll get job offers elsewhere. God is constantly at work, and he's not afraid to move people around.

The Gospels show us how Jesus pulled a team together. He poured himself into the lives of a first-century "staff." If we could have asked him about his greatest ministerial challenge, I think he would have said that it was leading those twelve men, keeping them focused and on the same page. And if Jesus faced this challenge, how much more will you and I struggle with it? Your team will be 100 percent human in makeup; no angels are taking job interviews these days. You'll have to work with flawed human beings (like yourself) who lose focus, who develop different visions, who get confused or angry or simply tired.

I'm often asked, "What single factor was your greatest advantage when you began to plant West Ridge Church?" I quickly reply that apart from the grace and power of God, it was the team around me—the three men and their families—that made the difference. Most of that staff is still present, and others have come alongside us since then. At all times, the team has been our greatest resource apart from God's leadership; leading, developing, and refreshing it have been among our greatest challenges.

Those of us from the original West Ridge team have all evolved in our responsibilities over nearly fifteen years of experience. Some have entirely different job descriptions. Most of the men who are currently on my staff leadership team—the smaller team that supervises the larger one—have been there for an average of less than three years. So yes, we're in almost constant transition. This means a certain number of difficult conversations, more than a few sleepless nights, and the kind of personal growth as a leader that can be hammered out only on the anvil of experience.

Invest heavily in building relationships with your staff. Many leaders work hard to maintain a "professional distance" from those they lead. But in order to nurture trust, respect, and authenticity, you should make the effort to be real and build a sense of community among your staff. This means making the appropriate emotional, social, and spiritual connections that enable you to know and develop their soul. Too many staff members do ministry side by side without ever knowing what fresh work God is doing in each other's lives.

— Mac and Cindy Lake,
LAUNCH Church Planting Network

It's Not about Me — or You

As I related in the previous chapter, I had a pivotal moment several years ago when I realized that, as Max Lucado said, *it's not about me*. More than ever, pastors need to understand that their churches don't revolve around them. If I build a church to revolve around my personality and special gifts, what will happen when I'm no longer there? We who follow Christ are not called to build a short-term memorial to ourselves; it should be a vessel for the work of God, built for eternity. If we do no more than brand ourselves and serve the result to an audience, we've served them fast food rather than the Bread of Life, sugar water rather than living water.

It's not about us. God and only God can get the glory, and all that we build must begin with that premise — particularly a team. If I have men and women on my team who are better known in the church world than I am, I won't be threatened by that; as a matter of fact, it will make me smile. If it doesn't have to be all about me, I can attract better leaders for my team. I meet people who are shocked that I still have team members who were with us from the beginning and that we've moved them around to different positions and even brought in *new* team members who supervise the old ones. Their eyebrows are raised as they ask, "How's that working out for you?"

The answer: pretty good, actually. We've worked to embed the theme "It's not about me" in our DNA. Check your egos at the door, because only God gets the credit here. "It's not about me, as the pastor," I tell the staff, "but it's not about you, as the team member, either." If we discover that someone could be more fruitful in a different capacity, we'll move them to a different place. Do we worry about their feelings? Yes and no: we try to do everything lovingly, with grace, but this is God's work. Moving people around is challenging. But if you've done your hiring based on character, you can be so much more flexible and efficient. To the extent that you can keep office politics out of your team dynamic, you'll create a healthy environment in which everyone has the same focus: glorifying God and keeping unity in the forefront.

A Compelling Vision

I think back over the people who have served on our team over the years, and here's what I realize: our best hires never even asked about salary until the very end of the hiring process. Why? They looked around and realized that, as the U.S. Navy says, "It's not a job; it's an adventure." You want the kind of team members who are drawn to a compelling and exciting vision rather than a salary and benefits package. During an interview, you can lay out what God has shown you about the future and watch their eyes. Do they pick up on the excitement?

At West Ridge, our compelling vision is that we are building the kingdom of God. It's not about numbers or this kind of program or that kind of creativity. It's certainly not about promoting me or any other personality. We believe that the hand of God is on us to do something for him that glorifies his name. We believe that any vision which is less than that will lead to a revolving door for your staff.

There are three distinctives to a vision based on building God's kingdom:

1. You'll know that the vision is truly from God, because it's all about him.

2. It will be a vision that is too much for you to handle in your own abilities or wisdom.

3. God will bring the right people to your team, and he'll keep them there long enough for you to make significant progress toward your goals.

When you have a compelling God-given vision, you must keep it constantly front and center with your team. Repetition helps to make it second nature for people, so you cast it over and over again. As you talk about specific initiatives and issues, you discuss them in light of how they connect to the overall vision. This inspires the team. They know it's not about business as usual but about being on the front lines of God's work in this world. That excites people; I know it does me.

Deep inside, all of us want to live out a great adventure; God has instilled that in us. People who can't find that will settle for lesser things: salary, benefits, comfort. But a vision that thrills the soul will captivate people. They will follow a compelling idea even beyond the point of sacrifice. For the chance to be part of something bigger than they are, they will put other things aside. They'll also stay with you longer, rather than always keeping an eye out for the next rung on the job ladder.

Jesus walked along the seashore and encountered men who had been fishing all their lives. He said, "Follow Me, and I will make you become fishers of men" (Mark 1:17 NKJV). They followed him from that day. They'd been casting their nets, but Jesus cast them a vision, and it filled their imagination. We read the story and ask, what would make a man throw down his tools and walk away with a stranger? The answer is, a compelling vision. Have you established one? Have you instilled it in your team?

Hire Your Superiors!

If you visit a staff meeting at West Ridge Church, I believe you'll agree with me that there's a lot of talent in the room. These men and women are all better than I would be in those particular roles. You can't imagine how much less stress you have to handle when you surround yourself with people who have supreme skills and a passion to use them.

There's something else too: seeing the quality of their work keeps me on my toes. It pushes me to be a better leader, because an excellent leader is necessary for leading excellent people. It's important to look for people who are passionate about their area of expertise — people you deeply respect.

This raises the question of hiring people who happen to be your friends. I recently heard a well-known pastor advise against hiring a close friend. I understand his point and acknowledge the things that can go wrong with that formula, but I hold a different view. Jesus's closest friends were part of his team, and that's the case with my team as well. The fact is that if you have a close friend, you probably already respect his or her gifts. You have good chemistry with that individual, and you already know that the two of you can work well together. Isn't it possible that God has brought both of you together so you can cooperate in doing his work? Obviously, it would be a bad idea to hire a friend *just* because of friendship, if better candidates are available. But if that person is excellent at the job where you have a vacancy, then it could be a game changer to have that friend on staff.

I love hanging out with skilled, proficient people. I soak up their passion and learn all kinds of things I never knew before. Being around high achievers increases my drive to achieve great results. It also makes me want to pour more of myself into them, doing anything I can to help them multiply their fruitfulness. On the other hand, here's a pattern we see too often, sadly enough: a senior pastor who has surrounded himself with people who are less gifted than he is. Oftentimes it comes out of insecurity; he doesn't want to feel threatened by other people's giftedness. The predictable result is that the senior pastor spends most of his time being irritated with his staff members, and so he has no friends among his staff. He feels more isolated than ever.

An insecure pastor feels the need to be the star at all times, the smartest guy in the room at staff meetings. He also wants to micromanage the various ministries. He can't do that when his team members have a state-of-the-art familiarity with their fields and are doing their work excellently. When the pastor must have his hand on every ministry and every decision, he will eventually become the lid to the church's growth. There are limits to his time and his talent, and those limits will define the church's limits. There will also be a revolving door on the staff as people leave in frustration. He may have wanted to own all the glory; he ends up owning all the problems.

The secure pastor, on the other hand, knows that there is only one star, and he reigns in heaven. This pastor wants the church to vastly transcend his personal limits of time and talent, so he surrounds himself with great leaders and allows them to fully invest their gifts for God's kingdom. He refuses to micromanage but instead gives his people the freedom to dream and be creative in their areas, and he trusts them with big decisions.

Hiring and Firing

I've heard several church leaders use this phrase: "Hire slowly, fire quickly."

What do they mean? Clearly, you want to be very thorough in the hiring process. By the time a new team member becomes part of your staff, you will have gotten to know this person well, understanding exactly how he or she will fit into the vision and values of your church. Bill Hybels offers three essentials for evaluating any potential addition to your team: character, competency, and chemistry. At West Ridge, we add a fourth: *calling.* We want to know that our candidate is not merely accepting a job but pursuing a divine calling to be part of what we're doing. As Amy likes to put it, we want raving fans of West Ridge Church.

We want a new team member to be very competent, but we also know there's always room for growth and improvement in competency. Chemistry will have to be developed, though we do want to hire people who fit well on our team. Character, on the other hand, is less flexible; either you have it or you don't. So we look very closely to try to make an evaluation here.

We take some time attempting to measure these four factors. But why fire quickly? At West Ridge, we talk a lot about vision and values. It's essential that every member of our team shares those. When it becomes clear that someone has a different vision or different values, they need to go—without delay. Otherwise there will be disruption and disunity, and the longer things are drawn out, the more damage will be done. No one likes to dismiss a staff member, particularly in a church setting. You can fire a bagger at the grocery store, and it won't cost the store any customers. But when church staff leave, people almost always leave with them. It can create controversy. You will be misunderstood, and it can be very personal when you are close friends.

I have struggled to let go of team members. I'm long-suffering, and when in doubt, I've chosen to err on the side of grace. I've been slow to act, sometimes to the detriment of the church. For what's at stake, I know that's wrong. Like every leader, however, I have my tipping point, and it's disunity. God's work is too important to allow for disunity. Hybels says that regardless of how loving and compassionate we are, when we refuse to deal with challenging personalities, we frustrate the productive team members. If someone is not a happy part of your team, release him, and you're doing the right thing for him as well as for your church.

How High Should I Fly?

Another common question concerns how much involvement the lead pastor or planter should have with day-to-day decisions. In the beginnings of West Ridge, I had my hands in everything. If you intend to plant a church, you'd better be prepared to be a jack-of-all-trades for a season: preach the sermons, answer the phone, sweep the floor, manage the finances, plan the publicity, or do whatever else needs to be done.

It's exhausting, but a planter can become too comfortable with being a one-man band. As time goes on and growth comes, it's important to be deliberate about pulling back and avoiding micromanagement. I use the illustration of flying in a plane over the broad sweep of our ministry. In the early days I would fly close to the ground. I could see most of what was going on, and I could swoop in and give an opinion or a word of guidance easily. I wasn't seeing every detail, but I had a good grasp of the whole picture. As we grew from several hundred in attendance to one thousand, I increased my altitude. Now I was about ten thousand feet high, and I could see the big picture, but a lot of the activities were harder to make out. The culture of the church was becoming more complex. As we grew toward three thousand in attendance, decisions and directions were developing without my knowledge. There's a moment when the pilot realizes that, and he feels a certain amount of vertigo. It's frightening to give up control, but otherwise his church will stop growing and reaching new people for Christ.

Moses faced such a crisis in the wilderness and found that the Israelites needed more structure; he couldn't be all things to all people anymore. The first-generation church faced such a crisis too, when the initial surge of growth came. Deacons were set forth to take care of things the Apostles could no longer personally handle.

We simply must learn to equip the saints and empower them to perform their ministries. It's all part of realizing that *it's not about you*. It's not just about your community. It's not just about your generation. It's about people and places and times that stretch far beyond us, until Christ returns. We can't afford to undermine the pattern Christ has set, by being so controlling that we become the lid to a church's potential.

West Ridge Church now has several thousand people attending

at three different locations. You'll learn a lot about letting go when you release people and leaders to a new location. As pastor, I suppose I'm hovering at about thirty thousand feet. I'm more of a big-picture guy than I once imagined I could be. I can see the lay of the land for a great distance. I know who the decision makers are, and I love and trust them, because there is no way I can personally minister to thousands of people.

I no longer even want to know what is going on in every Bible study group, every program, every mission. I may not be able to tell you who plays the drums this week over at the West Paulding location. But I'm very interested in information, progress, and people. I hear a report each week from every lead team member.

Still, every once in a while I'll peer through the clouds and spot something that doesn't look quite right; it doesn't line up with the vision and values of our church. So I'll once again turn the nose of my plane downward and swoop closer to ground level to engage. People aren't always happy to see my plane approaching in those situations, but I know that all the decisions, including the bad ones, come back to me eventually. My staff understands that.

They know I'm going to ask detailed questions occasionally and find out exactly whether they're adhering to our vision and values. But no matter how high or low I fly, I can limit those uncomfortable moments. The key is to be clear and consistent in sharing our vision and values. Then I have to understand, within the context of that vision, the size of the box in which each team member operates. When we say box, we're referring to the extent of what they're allowed to do. People with bigger gifts need bigger boxes.

If you find the right people, offer a satisfying range for ministry, and avoid micromanaging, you will keep great people on your team. You'll see them grow along with their ministries; they will outgrow their boxes and need bigger ones. But if you make the boxes small and confining, and you're always flying low, always looking over their shoulders, then you'll be spending a lot of time rehiring. I find that the boxes need to be different sizes and that there are some I need to be more involved in than others.

Where Does the Buck Stop?

Planting a church will involve more tough decisions than you could ever anticipate.

When we came to Atlanta as a team of four, we were young and idealistic. We had the idea that we would be a four-member democracy, all of us equal in every way. As each issue came to the fore, we would discuss it and make a decision on it together. It would always be this way, we assumed. We resisted ideas of structure, hierarchy, and set job descriptions. We wanted to be flexible. Our hearts were in the right place; we simply wanted to do church in a new way, as each generation does.

Tough times have a way of making us more realistic. It became clear that someone had to be the leader. Someone had to step up and make decisions, because if everyone is in charge, no one is in charge. We realized together that I had to be that person. It was a significant moment in the history of our church — painful in some ways but helpful in that we became better about applying our personal spiritual gifts to ministry. This, of course, is the biblical pattern: vision isn't something that's voted upon; it comes from God, and it moves forward through the different kinds of gifts he gives each of us.

Being the decision maker isn't a bed of roses. In my days of student ministry, I had no idea what it was like to carry the burden of a senior pastor. I used to hear Dr. Falwell say that "people don't know what this is all about until they sit on this side of the desk." The day came when I called him on the phone and said, "Dr. Falwell, I'm sorry."

He said, "What for?"

"I always had this idea that I might be able to do certain parts of your job better, if I were in your shoes. I was clueless!"

He laughed and said, "Brian, I knew you'd call me one day!"

I imagine I wasn't the first to make that confession to him. It's a shock to discover the feeling of carrying the weight of a church with your decisions. Dr. Falwell and I went on to have a great conversation about how to adjust to such a role.

We do things at West Ridge with a team of teams. We have a church staff team. We have an elder team that provides oversight and discernment to the church. We have a stewardship team that brings accountability to the use of finances and personnel at our church. There's a staff leadership team with whom I work on the daily decisions, and I have an accountability team of three elders whom I meet with monthly. As the title says, these men hold me accountable. These men speak deeply into my life and even have the authority to remove me from my position if need be.

But even with all these structures, at the end of the day I carry the final weight of things on my shoulders. It's a lonely place, and the larger the church grows, the greater the teams grow, the lonelier this position is. As Dr. Falwell said, you won't understand that until you sit on this side of the desk.

Do you shy away from big decisions? Are you uncomfortable with the buck stopping at your desk? It's something to consider as you get involved with planting a church, because over time the decisions go from small to medium to large to massive. You will have the opportunity to grow as your church grows, and God will prepare you to shoulder a bit more with each passing year. But it's important to consider from the outset whether you're emotionally, mentally, and spiritually tough enough to be the point man of your team.

Open Lines

There must be a decision maker, but there's a difference between a strong decision maker and a tyrant. While someone must sit in the driver's seat, that person should also be very comfortable with taking good advice. Communication is nearly always at the root of any struggling relationship, whether it be a marriage or a ministry. If you don't keep people up on things, they'll be down on things. I find that the members of my staff don't covet the role of the decision maker, but they do want to know what's going on and feel included. I'm the same way; I enjoy being in the loop, having enough information to feel that I have a good handle on the world around me.

I have an open-door policy with my whole team. It's important to me that each member feels he or she can come to say what should be said, as well as to hear what needs to be heard. I understand, of course, that communication is a two-way street. If I want my team members to confide in me, I need to confide in them.

In the story of the Tower of Babel, God says, "The people are united, and they all speak the same language. After this, nothing they set out to do will be impossible for them!" (Gen. 11:6 NLT). It's true—when we speak the same language, we are united; we are strong. In the narrative, of course, the goal was wrong, so God defeated the people's purpose by confounding their language. We believe that our unity toward a proper goal, empowered by the Holy Spirit, means results that please God.

There are so many problems with the way people communicate in churches. One of them comes when we assume that team members know certain facts. I've learned the hard way, too many times to mention, that it's never wise to assume. Our friend Chip Judd likes to say that when questions are left unanswered, Satan likes to fill in the blanks with lies and misinformation. We would rather take the risk of being repetitive. We don't mind seeing people's lips move along with us as we say certain key phrases — our vision and values, for example — because that means they know what we're talking about. Business experts will tell you that in any organization, you have to speak an important message multiple times before people truly hear it.

Try creating a system that provides information to your team on a weekly basis, with opportunity for feedback. Give it some thought, because it's harder than you think. Will people read your email carefully before hitting the delete button? Will they get the memo? Are they paying attention as the weekly calendar is read during the staff meeting, or are they daydreaming? Just because something has been said does not guarantee that it's been heard.

I may not have all the answers, but I do know where many of the questions come from: poor communication. As a church planter, you have the opportunity to build structures and systems that do a better job of getting the word out.

Protect the Environment

I notice that great church planters aren't necessarily great encouragers. Maybe it's because I see myself in this principle — I could be a better encourager than I am. I'm working at it; I think I do a better job now than I once did. I believe that if I'm going to swoop down from thirty thousand feet to fix things or give direction, then I can also swoop down to encourage and strengthen our people.

Planters are very interested in matters of strategy and structure. They'll read book after book about these issues, never thinking that they need to know the basics of relationships as well. I believe relationships are much more important. You might build a great machine, but you need to grease the wheels every now and then. In a church plant, where the machinery is going to heat up frequently, we grease the wheels with encouragement, love, and appreciation. We find that when we do that, the parts last much longer.

We work hard to create that environment on our team. Again, I think back to the early days, the crisis days, when we had that living room meeting and decided we would have each other's backs. But we do more than simply protect each other. We cheer each other on. We try to build positive, supportive relationships, and when someone does something right, we celebrate that and credit them publicly. We try to create that atmosphere on our team, then find that it spreads to the whole church. Isn't that what leadership is all about?

We all know that people watch the pastor's wife. They also watch the staff closely. They take in the body language, the facial expressions, the little cues that show whether this staff loves each other or not. When they do see that camaraderie, they believe our message. They know we are Christians by our love, as the old song says, and they're encouraged to a higher standard among themselves. When they see tension in the staff, their thoughts are, *This is just like the office where I work — no different at all. There's conflict, office politics ... I had really hoped it could be different in God's church.*

I'd like to offer five ways to express love and gratitude to your team.

1. Share the glory with them whenever possible. Say their names in public.
2. Celebrate the wins, showing your team that you appreciate their contribution.
3. Make the office a fun and positive place in which to work.
4. Do what it takes to heal conflicts.
5. Be transparent. Let your team members see your heart.

Great teams build great churches! It all starts and ends with your willingness to grow as leader.

How do you deal with baggage or past abuse in your own life while leading a church?

The rigors of planting a church and leadership will eventually surface whatever weak spots there are in your character, including the shrapnel that has been left from past hurts. Sooner or later you'll meet someone in your church or lead someone on your team who will embody and reintroduce you to past wounds and the struggles you thought you had left behind. The pain in your past is a part of God's ultimate design for you as a leader. He allowed you to go through it back then so he can use it in your life now and do great things through you in the future. You must be vulnerable enough to get gut-level honest about these struggles. Find an appropriate mentor, counselor, or friend with whom to share your insecurities and fear. Keep your spouse in the loop and stay transparent in your day-to-day conversations and interactions. And whatever you do, let your past keep you humble before God. Refuse to let your past make you a bitter leader. Allow God to use it to make you a better leader!

— Jonathan and Donna Robbins,
The Summit Church, Winston Salem, NC

Questions to Think About

1. How Would You Evaluate Yourself as a Team Player?

Are you ready for the level of interdependency that will be brought by the rigors of planting a church? Are you comfortable with your strengths as well as your areas of need? You will need to recruit coworkers who share your passion for building this church, and you'll need to evaluate them closely. Are you a good judge of character? Are you effective in articulating the core values and the vision for what you wish to build?

2. Are You Comfortable with the Pressure of Making Difficult Decisions?

As you progress and as your church grows, the decisions will become increasingly complex. The pressures will intensify. How will you cope with the loneliness of sitting on that side of the desk? How would you describe your decision-making process during past issues of your life?

3. What Is Your Management Style? Are You an Effective Delegator?

Some planters are control freaks. They feel the need to be involved in all that goes on. This is possible only at the beginning of a church plant. As your church grows, will you be able to relinquish control over the various ministries? Then there is the big-picture issue. Can you fly over the landscape of a busy church and macromanage, with a solid staff of leaders?

4. Are You an Encourager?

Relationships are more important than strategy and structure — this is a key insight for church planters. You'll need to be a positive, encouraging leader. Does this role come naturally to you, or will it take some work? Do you believe you can create a fun and challenging work environment? Do you believe others will experience joy and fulfillment from working on your staff?

The quality of a staff team goes a long way toward determining the quality of a church. Assemble your dream team carefully, communicate clearly, relate lovingly, and as God has said, there's nothing you can't do. You'll go farther than you ever expected, and you'll enjoy the richest human fellowship available in this life.

CHAPTER 8

IS IT SAFE TO HAVE FRIENDSHIPS INSIDE AND OUTSIDE THE CHURCH?

Who Is in Your Circle?

Amy and I have a couple we consider to be some of our closest friends, Michael and Jenniffer Marblestone. Although we don't get to spend as much time with them as we would like, we value their friendship. In fact, they've taught us a lot about what it means to be a good friend. We've traveled with them on several occasions, and our kids have basically grown up together.

We'll never forget the first time the four of us went to dinner. It was Mexican food at a restaurant called On the Border. As we took our seats and placed our napkins in our laps, Jenniffer looked at us with a little blush and said, "I'm not really sure how to ask this."

"Ask what?" Amy urged.

"Well, um — is tonight a 'ministry' thing for you?" She made "air quotes" with her fingers as she said the word *ministry*. "Or are you just here because you're our friends?"

Amy and I started laughing. We'd never heard that question before. But other times, when it hadn't been spoken, we'd known it was floating in the air.

Our friend quickly said, "I hope I haven't said the wrong thing! But you know — are you guys, like, at *work*, or is this just for fun?" Amy and I both began reassuring them that they were truly our friends, that we would not be there if we didn't want to be. Yet it's a legitimate question, isn't it? Where do you draw the line between work and play?

Ministry isn't like a job, say, doing road construction. The guy who does that is never asked, "Are you officially at work, or are you just tearing up the street for fun right now?" A brain surgeon knows exactly when he's working and when he's not. But a pastor's work time can be a gray area. It often overlaps with another person's *free* time. The pastor is performing his job description when he delivers a sermon; the people in the audience are there because they felt like coming.

But what happens when someone throws a children's birthday party? What about an appearance at the neighborhood pool or the school soccer game? What about an informal dinner? Is the pastor on the clock at those events? Most people would say, "Oh, listen —when you're with us, you're among friends! Don't feel like you're on the job." People don't want to feel as if they're no more than a responsibility on your work agenda. They want to be friends with the nice people who make up their church staff team.

On the other hand, when Amy and I go to the neighborhood pool, it's not long before someone pulls over a deck chair and says, "Hey, Brian, I've been meaning to talk to you." Sometimes these conversations turn into a pastoral counseling session, the only difference being that the sun is out and you can get splashed. We love our people, so naturally we listen and respond in that situation.

The point is that a fun trip to the pool has become work time. Amy and the kids and I came to the pool simply to have some family fun, like anyone else. The line between friendship and ministry is blurred for those of us who are planting churches. And what's important is that the blurriness *extends to our relationships*. Were we having dinner with friends or ministering to church people?

Pastors and their spouses need friends, just like everyone else. How can we accomplish that in a church-planting context? We dearly love the people at West Ridge. They're cool and fun, and it hurts us that we can't hang out with all of them. What should we do when we want to be friends with thousands of people, but we know we have the ability to be good friends with only a few? As Amy and I work with planters across the country, we find that this question crops up frequently. These people are realizing that church planting can be very lonely; they've been around pastors who have become isolated and possibly discouraged. They're asking us, "How can I establish safe friendships? Can I have friends within the church? Or can I be close only to outsiders?"

Getting Real

When I was a young, single student pastor, I loved being invited to people's homes. I *knew* why I was there on those occasions — because I was hungry! It was one of the few ways I could enjoy a well-cooked meal. I had no wife or children, and it was nice to be in a family setting and sit at a dinner table.

Again, when we were launching West Ridge, we had a relatively small staff team for the first few months. We shared meals together all the time, and we often shared meals with new people who were coming into our church fellowship. The entire staff team had dinner together every week.

As we added another hundred people, then another thousand, things changed. The time came when we couldn't have dinner with everyone who attended, nor could we even handle a weekly staff dinner. There was just too much going on in our lives, particularly as our kids grew older and became more active. I've already related how I struggled with this transition. I always worried about how other people perceived me, always felt I was letting someone down. I know a lot of pastors who feel the same way, and in some cases their churches stop growing because of this discomfort. They may not see it this way, but they've chosen to keep their church at a size allowing them to personally feel loved and needed by each individual, *instead of* adjusting their expectations so they can keep reaching new people for Christ.

Pete Wilson of Cross Point Church in Nashville says, "As pastors get over their need to be loved, they can become loving." This is true for at least a couple of reasons. Number one, you'll love more people indirectly by empowering other people to reach them. You simply have to build more effective structures and systems (ministry teams, small groups, care ministries, and discipleship classes) to spread the love. If you put a lid on your church's growth, you can retain your claim of being "friends" with everyone who attends. But the cost? People who won't be reached, because of your perception that you don't have room for them. We can't afford to define the Great Commission by the number of names we can keep straight.

Number two, you'll do a better job of loving the people in your circle of intimacy, because if you spread yourself too thin, there

We believe Jesus' safe friends were Peter, James, and John. Dave Busby once referred to them as Jesus' garden friends. These were the three men who in some ways saw him at his best on the Mount of Transfiguration. They also saw him at his relative worst in the Garden of Gethsemane. We have found it a necessity to recognize and do life with people who aren't impressed with whatever perceived status we may have but also recognize and value the role God has given us to play in the local church. Rather than drain us, they laugh with us and refresh us. They are willing to kneel and pray with us in our weakest moments, knowing that we too face temptations and the fatigue of life. Our safe friends have been our garden friends.

— Larry (and Kathy) Grays,
lead pastor of Midtown Bridge Church, Atlanta, GA;
vice president of The Rebuild Initiative
Urban Church Planting Network

will be less of you for your spouse, less of you for your kids, less of you for your closest friends. Build more effective structures, and you'll love those in your circle far better. Get over your need to be loved by everybody, so you can truly love the realistic number of people God has built you to care for.

Work within Your Boundaries

Our first insight, then, is obvious: one person can have only so many friends. A church has to remain very small for you to be a good friend of everyone who attends it. You'll have to get comfortable with a certain number of people inevitably thinking you're aloof and unapproachable. You have to learn to say no to a certain number of invitations and demands.

God gave you a finite capability for friendships. You can have probably no more than seven true friends at a given time. How many truly *intimate* friends — a spouse or lifelong best friend — can we have? Even fewer. But there may be seven people who have your cell phone number, who know they can call you at any time, and with whom you can do the same.

Outside that circle is another one that may include 150 people. These are people you count as friends, people you easily interact with, people you schedule into your yearly calendar, though they're not as intimately close as those seven.

Finally, there is a circle outside that one; everyone else is in that circle. You're not responsible for being friends with all those people. What you can do is create a church that makes rewarding friendships possible for them through others. This is why we equip people for ministry.

Where did we get the idea that we have to interact equally with every person? It's simply not possible. Jesus interacted with a large group of people — the crowds that followed him, people he healed, Pharisees he rebuked. He had twelve men in his second circle, as he trained them and loved them. Then he had an inner circle of three men, Peter, James, and John—his intimate friends. In his hour of need, when his death approached, he chose these three to go to the garden with him. He didn't invite the rest of the world, or even the rest of the disciples. And when Jesus went to pray to his Father in the garden, he drew away even from the inner circle and spent time alone with the one relationship that mattered most of all—the one greatest Friend we all have.

Christianity is about radical love, but it's not about unrealistic expectations. If Jesus could be strategic in the way he handled his social relationships, so can we. Since the church started, Amy and I have made it a point to be part of teaching the membership class our church offers. This is a good choice for us, because it gives us an opportunity to meet with people in a smaller setting, before our church culture can offer them opportunities for ministry teams, small groups, and other things. We also enjoy visiting with various small groups in the church from time to time so we can get a taste of what God is doing among different groups of people.

The Art of Friend Finding

We have to recognize that loneliness—to some extent—comes with leadership. Still, we need friends. The solution is to be a little more deliberate about finding them. We're not meant to be alone, and what a cruel irony if a pastor and his or her spouse are the ones who starve the most for the love that only Christians can offer so thoroughly.

Let's mention first that your wisest choice of a best friend is the one whose name is next to yours on the marriage license. Your marriage should be romantic, and it may be a partnership in ministry, but it should also be the greatest friendship of your life. From time to time, Amy and I realize that we're in danger of becoming partners in church work at the expense of being best friends. We go and find something we both enjoy doing so we'll remember that we're much more than Mr. and Mrs. Ministry.

We also need an intimate friend or two who don't live in the same house we do. Could this person be a member of the church? It's not impossible. If so, it needs to be someone without an agenda, someone who needs nothing from us. For me, it will never be as close a friendship as the one my marriage offers, but it will offer that same-gender friendship (male for me, female for Amy) that everyone needs. I hope you have someone in your life like that, who has no agenda other than enjoying your companionship.

Sometimes we try to force a friendship, maybe with someone with whom it would be strategic to be friends. This usually doesn't work. The most powerful friendship is usually with someone who simply crossed your path, and you were drawn together by a unique chemistry — the kind of person you would have ended up hanging out with in high school, rooming with in college. You have common interests and have personalities that seem to naturally interlock. It's a good thing to ask God to bring you the right friend. He knows exactly the kind of friend you need.

> The pastor is the most connected person on the planet, but the loneliest. I (Ike) look for friends with integrity, and the greatest prediction of a person's future is to look at their track record. I like being around people who like being married, love their family, and love their church. I choose friends who share common interests and can rejoice with me when something good happens to me, without being jealous.
>
> — Ike and Robin Reighard,
> **Piedmont Baptist Church, Marietta, GA**

Friendships among Staff Wives

When I (Amy) have had the privilege of spending time with other church planters' wives, the topic of staff wives has almost always come up. "What are you doing with your staff wives?" we ask each other. I can tell you that most lead pastors' wives care for all the women and wives on their staff but are often challenged by how much time and responsibility they should take to connect them to each other. Should they have Bible studies, lunches, "Secret Sisters," or retreats? Should they feel obligated to open their home on a regular basis to host staff wife events?

Our first staff wife "event" involved the four of us girls going to Waffle King in the north Georgia mountains. A lot has happened since then, and now we have approximately forty wives, some of whom I barely know. Now we get together three or four times a year for lunches or holiday parties. My goal with our staff wives and the women on staff at West Ridge is to let them know that I care and that I'm available. I learned from my friend Emily Morgan that naturally occurring friendships seem to work best. When God knows I'm available, he seems to put someone on my mind repeatedly. It's then that I know that I need to somehow connect with that person.

There are also times when I feel overwhelmed, and I don't know who I'm supposed to reach out to with so many people and so many needs. So I just pray and ask God to guide me. I've learned that the friendships that work best for me are the ones with people who have the most in common with what's happening in my life: someone who lives nearby, someone whose kids are the same age as mine. I can relax and allow each friendship to be a blessing that comes in its own way and its own time, rather than just another part of church ministry that I have to force.

My best friend will always be my husband, and no one else

will come in better than a distant second place. But I need my girlfriends, and I'm grateful to God that he takes care of me by placing wonderful friends in my life.

The Friend-some Foursome

My (Brian's) good friend Ike Reighard suggests that every pastor needs at least four types of friends. First is the Developer, that friend who makes you a better person. If you look into the life of any truly effective and fruitful leader, you're going to find key people in the background who have poured themselves into this individual and helped to develop his gifts and abilities. They're natural encouragers, and who needs constant encouragement more than a pastor? In fact, pastors need encouragement and validation more than most people realize. Is there a Developer in your life who lifts you up whenever you fall down, who believes in you during times when you don't believe in yourself?

Second, there is the Designer. He also goes by the name of mentor — a hands-on, step-by-step coach for everyday life and work. Jesus, of course, was the ultimate mentor. The men he guided changed the world, and they did it largely by reaching out to mentor others in the way Jesus had done for them. Church history tells us that the Apostles were each surrounded by young disciples who absorbed their teaching. Paul mentored Timothy and several other younger men who became his protégés. Clearly, mentoring is a biblical path for passing on wisdom to the next generation. You need one. And here's a thought: you also need to be one. Every leader needs both a Paul and a Timothy.

A mentor will talk to you about any part of your life: marriage, ministry, parenting, business, emotions — any area in which you can say, "I'm struggling with this. Tell me what you've done about it in the past." They can live down the street or in another country;

even in the ancient world, Paul mentored Timothy across great distances. Reighard even points out that mentors can be dead. Dr. Bill Bright, founder of Campus Crusade for Christ (now Cru), was mentored by writers such as A. W. Tozer and Oswald Chambers. But the best mentors are people you can call on the phone or reach via text message in an hour of need. Do you have a Designer in your life? Where do you go when you lack wisdom?

Third, the Disturber is the guy who rocks your boat. He's there not to comfort you when you're afflicted but to afflict you when you're comfortable. He asks you the hard questions, calls you out when you're taking the easy way too much, and generally offers you the reality check you need in a world of hangers-on who will tell you only what you want to hear. The Old Testament prophets were clearly Disturbers for kings; so was John the Baptist. They said what needed to be said, even when it didn't help their popularity. God uses Disturbers to help us break out of our comfort zones.

Finally, there is the Discerner. He also goes by the name of accountability partner. This is a tough one, because accountability requires vulnerability in two directions. The Discerner finds the holes in your life and helps you fill them, and you do the same for him. There is a much higher level of intimacy than with the Disturber; you're more likely to confide your secrets to the Discerner.

I believe there are some friends who may embody two or even three of these aspects of friendship. The great danger is in limiting ourselves to feel-good friends. Pastors, often living in elevated stress, are susceptible to finding these and surrounding themselves with them. But pastors need all the angles that friendship has to offer. Which of these four do you lack?

Outside the Walls

We've discovered that it's very important for church planters to maintain friendships outside the church. As I mentioned before, a mentor relationship is a good example of a friendship that can be maintained over a great distance, while deeply enriching your life.

One of the advantages of modern times is that we have so many forms of technology that make geography less of a barrier. Once we had to pick up a pen and write letters, as Paul and Timothy did. Then there was the phone, then email. Now we have Skype and FaceTime and other methods of keeping up with each other. When we commission people to go overseas to do mission work, it's wonderful to know they don't have to be cut off from their homeland the way missionaries once were.

Yet the church planter often cuts himself off as if he had landed on some unexplored island in the South Pacific long ago. It happens because he becomes deeply immersed in the work of building a church. He puts in long hours, performs all kinds of tasks, and in the end he leaves no margin in his life for friendship or simply caring for his own needs. What happens when he needs to let off a little steam? Can he keep venting to his spouse, when she is sharing those same struggles? Where does *she* go to vent?

This is why we need to maintain and nurture the existing friendships we brought with us. These friends can be from past churches, can be from college or seminary, or can even be our brothers and sisters. We need friends who have known us well, who have proven their commitment to us, and who have no agenda other than just being our friends. It doesn't hurt to find a few new friendships, either, and these can be strategic: people who know exactly what we're experiencing, because they are too. We're learning to reach out to people who have similar tasks in ministry so we can help each other out. I've found that other pastors have been amazingly generous with their time and help. There are now so many good channels for networking among church planters that it's sad to imagine people not taking advantage of them.

I've mentioned in this book some of the names of Christian pastors and leaders I've taken the initiative to contact, and they've invariably been difference makers in my life. One of them helped me with this very issue of friendship. I got on a plane to Fort Lauderdale, Florida, and there visited Pastor Bob Coy of Calvary Chapel. I knew he was a loving, shepherding pastor, and I had come to a place where I saw friendship as a big issue in my life. He helped me to reconcile a lot of my anxieties about this, to realize my limitations and also what I needed to do to set boundaries in order to have healthy friendships.

Some of our close friends are pastors and their wives who live in other states. Although it's often a scheduling challenge, our time spent with those friends is invaluable because they get it. They get us. They get what we do. We have so much in common; even our kids have an instant bond. With friends like that, you can relax and be yourself—and oftentimes glean from their experiences.

It really helps to know you're not the only person in the world facing your particular problems. I encourage every planter to reach out to people who are in similar situations. If you're planting an inner-city church, find a network of others with that same specialty. If you're in the Pacific Northwest or West Texas or New York City, network with people who are in those same areas and who face similar challenges.

Church planter networks are now appearing online, with bulletin boards allowing people to interact, share problems, discuss solutions, and encourage one another. Amy speaks highly of *Leading and Loving It (leadingandlovingit.com)*, a website created by Lori Wilhite. It's a site for "connecting, equipping, and encouraging pastors' wives and women in ministry." Virtual community groups there are created for specific situations, and women are finding this site to be a safe place to come and find friendship and support. Our church-planting network called LAUNCH has created a Facebook community to connect women. We also have virtual church planting small groups to connect pastors' wives.

In the Community

Our family came to the metropolitan Atlanta area with a sense of calling to this corner of the world. In a sense, West Ridge Church isn't our true calling; the community is, specifically the *lostness* of the community. West Ridge is our response to that lostness, through God's leading. That means we refuse to disappear into the bubble of church culture. We invest in the community as much as we can, building friendships with people who may never attend a service at our church. Much of this, of course, revolves around our boys' activities, at school and in sports. I've coached both my sons in baseball, and we've gotten to know parents through Taylor and Zach's involvement in other sports and through their classes at school. We talk to our boys frequently about being a missionary family, and they'll be quick to tell you that they feel a calling to their school. It's a great way to get them involved in ministry from an early age. It's not simply their calling as pastor's kids; it's the calling that all believers have in this world.

As a result of our community involvement, we have friends who not only don't attend our church but also in many cases don't even know what I do for a living. It's a great way for me to have local friendships without the pressure of being someone's pastor. Maybe by the time they get to know my vocation, we will have earned their friendship, and they will know that we care about them enough to make them think seriously about what they may be missing spiritually. We are strategically cultivating friendships with unsaved people all the time.

I'll admit that it's a bit of a strain for our boys at times. We're very supportive of Christian schools and homeschooling, but for now we've elected to leave our boys in public schools, because we feel it's the right place for them to be and because we feel called to that specific community. (We reevaluate the situation each year, again with the priority of putting our kids' welfare first.) It's a real exercise in being in the world but not of the world, and I would simply summarize by saying that every family in ministry must decide for itself how to handle the school issue in a culture whose values are increasingly off-kilter.

We're committed to being "salt and light" for northwest Atlanta, and, as Jesus said, it makes no sense to hide our light under a bowl (Matt. 5:14–16). Jesus himself modeled this, reaching out to the people whom the religious types avoided. He was criticized for the parties he went to and the lost people he counted as friends. His critics didn't understand that this was the very reason he came into the world. He said, "It is not the healthy who need a doctor, but the sick. I have not come to call the righteous, but sinners" (Mark 2:17).

We can't follow his lead when we build our lives around a packed schedule of church activities. I might be criticized for being at my son's baseball game rather than a West Ridge event, but I'm ultimately accountable to one person, and he's the one I'm imitating.

Modeling Servanthood

I want to add one more thought before we leave this subject of friendship. One of the hot topics in church leadership discussions today concerns how much honor the pastor should receive. In some growing churches, pastors have a lot of perks lavished on them — top-of-the-line cars, CEO-level office suites, designer clothing. In some cases, pastors themselves have created the rock star environment. In some cultures, there is the notion that the church leader should be a role model of godly success — someone who has obeyed God and is therefore worthy of earthly rewards.

I understand these things, but I keep coming back to the image of Jesus kneeling before his disciples, taking their road-grimed feet in his hands, and washing them with water. The disciples were shocked; they felt it was unseemly for the Master to wash the feet of peasants such as themselves. They also thought that little children should be kept out of Jesus's path as he walked from village to village. He rebuked his friends and took time to gather the children into his arms. Jesus didn't simply go into the community; he *stooped to serve* the community—and he never set himself up as a rock star.

This is just a reminder that as we deal with our friends in and out of church, we need to remember that we are called to serve, not to be served. Occasionally people offer sports tickets or share a restaurant gift card with the pastor's family. We can gratefully accept friendly gifts, but we should never come to believe we're entitled to constant extras. We need to try the following words on for size: "How can I serve you today? What can I pray about for you?" And as we are blessed, we need to be giving generously to others.

I realized a long time ago that I could have only a few close friends and that as our church grew, I couldn't know everybody, couldn't have dinner with every family. I realized I couldn't do something for everyone, but I could do something for *someone*. Therefore I make it a goal to make a difference in one person's life every day. Whose life? I leave that to God. But as I talk to him in the morning, I pray, "Lord, let me make a positive difference in someone's life today. You show me the person and the time."

I've had to learn to be open to God interrupting my day. And he does. Maybe it comes when I'm putting gasoline in the truck. Maybe it comes at my son's game or as I say hello to a neighbor and listen carefully to hear a need mentioned. I'm going to live my life on the alert for any opening to bless someone at least in a small way. I think that's what friendship is all about at the end of the day, for the pastor and for his people: being willing to serve. What would your community look like if your church filled it with full-time servants?

Questions to Think About

1. Who Are Your Closest Friends?

It's very easy to become so absorbed in church planting that we don't tend to our own needs. You can probably name a close friend, but how active is that friendship? How frequently do the two of you catch up or spend time together?

It's a good idea to sit down and make a list of the starting lineup of your life, the seven or so people in your inner circle who have access to you all the time. Just as you need to surround your church life with a staff of capable, conscientious workers, you need to surround your personal life with loving, attentive friends who allow you to be exactly who you are.

2. Considering Reighard's Four Friend Types, Who Fills Each of Those Roles for You?

Ike Reighard says that every pastor needs at least one of each type of friend. Review his list and think about the roles your friends play. Even if some of your friends play more than one role, you need someone who majors in each of these. For example, do you have a true mentor? If you don't, who could you approach to consider that role? Do you have an accountability team or partner?

Having friends is important, but having a strategic balance of *kinds* of friends is vastly underrated.

3. How Effective Is Your Spouse's Friendship Circle?

Remember, the spouse of a church planter can be very lonely —even if your marriage and friendship are strong. Talk to your spouse, asking him or her to respond to question 1 above. What friendship needs are there? What can you do to help?

4. Have You Built Strong Community Relationships?

This is a goal for the entire church, and the pastor should take the lead. Your church is there to serve the community, for the sake of bringing the gospel to that community, not to be a gated fortress within it. This question should burn inside you: If your church ceased to exist, would your community mourn its loss? Wouldn't it be nice to think that your church provides so much positive value to its corner of the world that your community would grieve if it were gone?

If you haven't found opportunities to interact with schools, youth leagues, public servants, and other mainstays of your community, start working on that immediately. Some church planters are offering their services as chaplains to the fire department and police. Other new churches are organizing volunteer groups to clean parks and work concession stands at sporting events.

When we opened our church building, we gave oversized keys for our church to our county commissioner and our school superintendent. It was to symbolize that our building belongs to the community and that we were there to serve them. Schools have their football banquets and baccalaureates in our building. We host community and business meetings in our facilities for the purpose of leadership development.

We need to get beyond a reputation limited to "that church that creates a traffic hazard over on the main road." We do that by creating a church value of strong community service — and as you lead, your people will follow.

CHAPTER 9

CAN YOU REMAIN AUTHENTIC IN MINISTRY?

No One Can Be You
Better Than You

One of the values of our church is authenticity—being honest and open about who you are and comfortable with who God made you to be.

Our son Zach is a ton of fun. He is driven, outspoken, sensitive, and compassionate. In 2005 we discovered that he has ADHD—attention deficit hyperactivity disorder. Depending on which report you believe, anywhere from 5 percent to 9 percent of our schoolchildren are affected by ADHD. The psychologist told us that ADHD is common and it's hereditary. He went on to educate us on all the symptoms of the condition and the various strategies for dealing with it. We felt good about having a better understanding of our son and how his mind works. As we drove home, Amy and I talked over the symptoms and compared them with Zach's behavior. It all sounded very familiar. What startled me was that the symptoms didn't just paint a picture of Zachary; they had me nailed as well!

Thinking about Zach's ADHD became a supreme aha moment for me.

The well-known Peter Principle says that in any organization, leaders tend to rise to their level of incompetence. In other words, they excel where they are, and they continue to get promoted until they reach the level where they can no longer excel—their level of incompetence. I was at a place where I was beginning to ask the question, has this happened to me? I was feeling as if I had become the lid on our church's growth. West Ridge had grown to be a large church — maybe a size I wasn't capable of pastoring.

Ministry details were driving me crazy. I felt as if I had hit a wall, and I could not figure out how to navigate around it. Worse, someone told Amy that when they first met me, they were telling me their story, and I turned around and walked away. Imagine how I felt when I heard that I was walking away from people who were sharing their emotions! I said, "Tell me that didn't happen!"

But I knew it had. People with ADD (attention deficit disorder) will tell you that their mind is like a three-ring circus, where several thoughts and ideas are going on at the same time. So it's difficult to stay focused on one thing unless it is extremely stimulating to your mind. As you can imagine, it's difficult to go to sleep, and more difficult to stay asleep, when your mind is constantly racing. My staff would often joke about my inability to focus on details. But to know that I was actually walking away from people in midsentence was totally unacceptable. I told Amy, "I'm going to be tested for ADD, including an IQ test. If the psychologist tells me I don't have ADD, I'm just an idiot, then I'm going to resign, because West Ridge deserves a better leader."

The doctor brought in the results and smiled when he heard me speculating that I just might be an idiot. "Don't worry, Brian," he said. "You're actually very intelligent, and you're creative — which is very typical of people with ADD. Because ADD is definitely what you have." I cannot tell you how relieved I was at that moment. It helped bring a lot of my past and my present life into perspective.

ADD, a subtype of ADHD, is officially ADHD-PI, with the PI standing for "predominantly inattentive." This variation is often slower to be diagnosed because it lacks the hyperactivity factor. When younger children cause disruption because they can't sit still, their condition is more likely to be recognized. Those of us with ADD can remain in our seats and muddle through, but we go through life without knowing what it's like to think in an organized, focused way or to stay on track with a sustained conversation.

I had grown up with the belief that I was a people person, an extrovert with the ability to navigate through a challenging situation, but that I would always have to compensate for not being particularly smart, even though I made good grades. Getting diagnosed and treated was an incredible game changer for every aspect of my life. Good news — I wasn't an idiot! I just had, let's say, alternate wiring. And there were things that could be done to help me rein in my very active mind and be more productive in the situations a pastor must handle. Today I'm able to be more attentive with my family and with people in my church. I can remember sitting in a Starbucks with Amy, almost in tears in my new discovery of what it was like simply to have a focused conversation — and to remember where I put my keys.

I can't tell you how many church planters I know who suffer from ADD or ADHD without ever taking care of it. Why do they end up in this field? It's because people with ADD/ADHD are adrenaline junkies. They thrive on excitement, risks, and constantly renewed challenges. The first days of church planting are just right for them. They can be on the go, multitasking and avoiding the settled, organized, more everyday nature of established churches. But the time comes when they *do* have to sit in on a few meetings. They have to learn to value process. Sometimes they actually have to listen to people and stay focused on conversations that are not stimulating to their brain.

People with ADD/ADHD oftentimes live on a roller coaster, with emotional highs and lows. They need the next rush, the next shot of adrenaline, and when things settle down, they bottom out. In desperation, they may find themselves chasing the highs. They can make high-risk moves that are inadvisable. They can even create disruptions in their personal relationships.

As we talk to church planters, we warn them about these things. They may not have ADD or ADHD, but the point is that they need to *know themselves*, and know themselves well. In the long run, leading a church is going to require a high level of personal authenticity. That means we need to be honest about who we are, what we do well, what we don't do well, and what kind of structures need to be built around us to maximize our leadership abilities.

Taking Off the Mask

There can't be a larger cliché than the words *be yourself*. It's a no-brainer. Why is it, then, that many church planters struggle to know exactly who they are and to be comfortable in their own skin?

I believe that a great number of people who go into ministry may be insecure. They are verbal, articulate people who crave the validation of standing before a crowd and then being told they delivered a great sermon. Perhaps they're not entirely comfortable with who they are in Christ and what gifts they have. They're working hard to please people, because if they do that, people will validate their leadership. Therefore the planter is constantly straining to be his best self and to cover up the parts of his identity he is uncomfortable with and fears he might be rejected. He is, as we say, on all the time — performing, playing a role, auditioning for approval. This is a very tiring way to live, and it creates a lot of emotional problems.

Sometimes the planter may be emulating another pastor or leader he admires. This is just human nature when we're new in ministry. Writers emulate the styles of their favorite authors. Musicians sound a lot like the bands and artists that inspire them. A young leader looks at someone who has been successful and thinks, *If I do things exactly like this leader does, I'll be successful too.* In some cases, he even "borrows" sermons from the pastor he admires. He might pick up his mannerisms, and he'll be in a hurry to add new programs in his church just because his inspirational model has. In the previous chapter, we discussed mentoring, which is not the same as mere imitation. A mentor offers wisdom and speaks into our life and gifts. When we emulate someone, we merely use them as a template and hope for the same results.

I've had various mentors as well as models, and I've tried not to simply replicate their messages and mannerisms and strategies. But it's easy to get caught up in admiration for someone who embodies all that we want to accomplish. When we first went into church planting, in the midnineties, many guys wanted to be Bill Hybels or Rick Warren. I really admired Warren's model of the purpose-driven church, and we followed his lead in many ways. We felt it was a good fit for what God was doing in our lives at the time. But I blush slightly to admit that for a while I joined the Hawaiian shirt craze (that style being one of Rick's trademarks). A few of our people would say, "Here comes Hawaiian Brian." I suppose I was slightly self-conscious about getting the look right. Finally one day Amy put her foot down. She wrinkled her nose and said, "I am *over* those shirts, Brian. That's *not* who you are. And this isn't Orange County, California, and you're not Rick Warren."

And I knew she was right. As I began to grow and mature a little more, I became more in tune with what I had to offer that was unique and with how I should speak and lead and even look. I don't think there's anything wrong with gleaning from the preeminent speakers and leaders of our time. I even think we can pick up on and advance some of their insights into Scripture and our world, as long as we give credit and avoid plagiarism.

But at the end of the day, I've learned to be content with who I am as God made me. I'm a blue-collar guy who grew up in the outskirts of Detroit and was called to northwest Atlanta. If I can embrace that, then I'm embracing the fact that God does good work. He knew what he was doing when he made me good at certain things and not so good at others. Having ADD means that I think differently, and I may have to compensate for that. But it also means I'm more likely to be energetic and creative and to bring ideas to the table that someone else might not. If I have some flaw, that's just the flip side of a coin that has something positive on its other face. None of us can have every talent and advantage. Every talent has a flip side, and we have to take our abilities with our nonabilities.

I reached a point at which I became comfortable with not being Andy Stanley, Bill Hybels, Craig Groeschel, Francis Chan, or Rick Warren. But God didn't call any of those people to pastor a church in Dallas, Georgia; he called me here. I trust God to give me everything I need for serving him in the place to which he has led me. In the long run, my self-esteem and security are based in

How can you maintain authenticity while planting a church?

To get a church off the ground isn't a sprint but a marathon that demands nonstop, tremendous energy. Your success is dependent on your ability to build a team and keep them motivated — including your family, the most important team of all. The only thing that should determine who you are and what you do and how you relate to others is Jesus. Yet often in the drive of starting the new church, if you don't remind yourself of that, people and even team building become part of your "success" in driving the church, instead of discipling people and engaging the city. We have found three key things that keep it real and authentic with God, ourselves, and others. First is daily prayer. Prayer shouldn't be focused on your "project" or "ministry" but on your relationship with God. That doesn't mean you don't pray about challenges and opportunities, but it starts with loving Jesus, and what God thinks about me. That's the only opinion that matters. And he thinks enough of me that he sent his Son to die for me. Once I accept that God accepts me for who he made me to be and that he gave me everything I need, I can give more of myself to the calling he wants me to fulfill.

Knowing Our Weak Places

Another aspect of learning to be yourself is learning what your "besetting sins," or particular temptations, are. Satan doesn't use the same strategy for every human being. My weak places are going to be different than yours. It becomes very important that we realize exactly where they are, so we can keep watch and take measures to protect ourselves.

It's useful to look at yourself from the outside, from Satan's point of view. If you were he, what would be your point of attack?

it has to end there in our prayer, or we become gadgets to work the big church widget machine. Second is being honest when you preach and share about your failures, disappointments, and faults in life. It lets people see your humanity, and instead of being a superstar in their eyes, you are a human being doing all you can to follow Jesus. Third is having fun with the family. For us, having a sacred play day weekly — Saturday — to play with our kids was critical. We were broke but would do stupid stuff like riding the tram for free at the DFW Airport; when the kids would get loud, thinking it was an amusement ride, we'd just tell everyone we were from Arkansas on our way to vacation in Dallas! Taking time centers you, enforcing that you have a spouse and kids who need you as much as anyone.

— Bob and Nikki Roberts,
Northwood Church, Keller, TX

We know, for example, that vast numbers of pastors struggle with pornography addictions. Some wrestle with substance abuse. We have no way of measuring how many face much more "ordinary" obstacles: low self-esteem, marriages on the rocks, chronic depression. More generally, you can bet that if you're involved in any kind of spiritual leadership, the most basic temptations will involve either pride, pleasure, or power; those are Satan's same old tricks.

I hope you can see that it's vital for us to view ourselves holistically and unflinchingly, being bold enough to take a hard look at the places within us that are difficult to face. The Holy Spirit is our friend and guide in helping us know ourselves. The psalmist writes, "Search me, God, and know my heart; test me and know my anxious thoughts. See if there is any offensive way in me, and lead me in the way everlasting" (Ps. 139:23 – 24). God's Spirit will show you your weaknesses, but he will never point the accusing finger. Instead, he will show you with love and forgiveness. He will encourage you and strengthen you to stand firm in his power, and he will remind you that because of Jesus, you are an overcomer.

It's also important to have accountability partners — close personal friends with whom we can pray, confess, and find support. As I mentioned earlier, I meet with three elders monthly for accountability. Beyond that, we need to remember that there is no stigma associated with seeing a qualified counselor, someone with the insight and skills to help you understand your limitations and how to cope with them. A counselor changed my life when he helped me understand that I have ADD. Some planters are too busy to get the help they need or even to stop long enough to take stock of who they are and what challenges they're facing. That's the recipe for eventually hitting a wall. It's a lot wiser to do the right thing now, rather than atone for failure later.

Once we know our weaknesses, we must have a plan for coping with them, just as if we were going into battle — for of course that's exactly what we're doing. It's a matter of spiritual warfare. Satan isn't interested in tripping you up just because he has it in for you; he knows that through you he can negatively impact all the people you minister to. Rest is essential. Prayer is crucial. And you can't do these things whenever you happen to find a moment; you have to be deliberate and disciplined about them. I know, for example, that Monday morning is a wide-open door for temptation in my life, as it is for many pastors. That's when I'm drained. They call Monday morning the "holy hangover." Therefore my soul is on red alert on Monday morning. When I get up, I go for a run or to the gym and have a good workout, which is as good for me emotionally as it is spiritually. It enhances the connection between body and mind; it gets my blood flowing and keeps my thoughts from wandering. I listen to worship music and set my heart on God.

On Sunday nights, our church usually doesn't have a service or special event. I leave the morning service wired, adrenaline flowing from speaking. After we eat together as a family and get a little rest, that's when I would be tempted to overanalyze my sermon or brood over people's comments or whether I felt they responded as I wanted them to. All of that is God's business. Once I've delivered a sermon, it's up to his Spirit to move people and apply it to their lives. It's not about me. Therefore we do something fun as a family on Sunday evening. That's just part of my plan to minimize both my weaknesses and the way I know Satan likes to come at me.

As my life partner, Amy knows my points of vulnerability as well as I do, and I know hers. We keep watch on each other, and I could never count the number of times God has used us to help protect each other. As we've said more than once, planting a church will magnify every weakness you have. It will sift you. This is why it's so important that you know who you are, where the thin places in your armor are found, and what the best plan is to fortify them.

Avoid the Rock Star Trap

A special danger for the church planter is the temptation of pride. We live in an age of branding, where people are encouraged to think of themselves as products to be marketed. There are some excellent advantages in intelligently promoting a church or a ministry, but we can't get personally caught up in it on an ego level.

I see planters becoming engrossed in social media, for example. This is fine, up to a point. I use Twitter; our church uses Facebook. These services are neither good nor evil, just modern media for specialized communication. But what happens when those of us in ministry begin to find our significance in how many people are following us through Twitter or retweeting attention-getting compliments? I'm seeing this happen. Planters are engrossed in the idea of creating Internet identities. After a while, they're so engaged in vast Twitter conversations over this or that, that they don't realize they're doing a lot less flesh-and-blood ministry.

Having followers on Twitter or getting your like button clicked on Facebook becomes one more path of validation. It's the rock star syndrome, the seduction of image polishing. At the same time, denominations and planting networks are spotlighting people who have experienced some success, and this just makes the ego trap that much more dangerous. It's just another hook that can be used to separate us from the real purpose of what we're called to do: make disciples.

Where does all this name-centric activity lead? Over the last few years, Amy and I have seen friends in ministry deal with moral failure. It's heartbreaking to sit and talk with them, to hear their regrets. Every church planter — every pastor, for that matter — should sit and listen to such a conversation. These are highly gifted people who got into ministry for all the right reasons, worked hard, built ministries that God blessed, and then simply crashed because somehow it became about them instead of bringing glory to God.

We once admired a well-known pastor who had an affair that ruined his ministry. A friend of ours talked to him and asked him the obvious question: How could he know the Bible so well, be a minister of the gospel for so long, and think he could escape the consequences of such serious sin? The pastor replied, "Because God was blessing my ministry, I thought that he was giving me a pass on my sin." God doesn't give passes. He has no tolerance at all for sin; otherwise he never would have sent his Son to die as a response to our sin problem.

Perhaps you can't imagine yourself falling into an extramarital affair. Maybe it couldn't happen to you today or next week. But as a human being, you can be confident that there is a weak place somewhere in your armor. There is an opening for sin to begin its

In an urban setting you can't be fake when your neighbors can hear you through the walls. We have come to understand that the people in our city are always watching and that attention becomes a stewardship issue for us. The realization that you are under constant surveillance forces you to wrestle hour by hour throughout your day with the image of God you are displaying. In other words, there are no pedestals, no one who admires a pastor for the position. People only value witnessing faith, hope, and love. Having so many people in such a small area allows us to interact with our neighbors on nearly a daily basis. As a result, we want our neighbors to believe that we are the best neighbors, that we love God and love our church family — and they are welcome to join us in that family.

— Ellis and Ginger Prince,
Gallery Church, Baltimore, MD

work. There is some form of desire—for pleasure, for power, for pride of accomplishment. Pure and clean desire is a godly thing, but it can be twisted. James 1:15 tells us that "after desire has conceived, it gives birth to sin; and sin, when it is full-grown, gives birth to death." We have seen the death of great ministries because people simply didn't take the time to honestly deal with issues of the heart, to set up boundaries where they were at risk, and to invite God and others into their situation to help them deal with it.

Off the Pedestal

Being authentic means protecting your name and image from becoming inflated by your church or by anyone else—in other words, keeping the church from putting you on a pedestal.

There's a school of thought in the Christian world that the easiest way to build a church is on the basis of a powerful personality. Just as you'd build a professional sports team on a franchise player —an athlete who causes tickets to be sold—the idea is to bring in the personality with the right charisma, and that will fill the church. That's a long way from the church planters who secure an elementary school cafeteria and walk from door to door, as we did, hoping someone will show up to have church with them. Nobody in Paulding County had ever heard of me. So I wasn't too concerned about being put on a pedestal. And now, after fifteen years, we still want West Ridge to be all about Jesus.

It's Jesus's church. It's the people of northwest Atlanta's church. Even though the church is a reflection of God's work inside us, the Holy Spirit is drawing people into salvation, discipleship, and fellowship. Those of us on the staff are just parts of the body of Christ, using our gifts. This is the biblical viewpoint, and it's the only one we can afford to wrap our minds around. Therefore we have to create a culture that doesn't make the pastor the center of everything. It's important to put the spotlight on Christ *all* the time, because he's the only one worthy to be illuminated by it. We are merely the stagehands who operate the spotlight.

People will see you as authentic and real if they experience you as a part of the community — a regular guy. For about nine years, I coached baseball for the teams my boys were on. When I was seen driving around the community in my cap and jersey, people could understand that I didn't descend from some cloud each week to preach a sermon; I was a Paulding County guy like everyone else. Sometimes, on the back of my jersey, instead of "Coach," I would have "Zach's Dad" or "Taylor's Dad" spelled out. I didn't advertise West Ridge Church in that space. (Unfortunately, Amy had a jersey that identified her as "Taylor's Mom," and I grabbed it and put it on one day when I was in a hurry. I'll never live that one down.)

We have established authenticity as a value at West Ridge Church. If the pastor demonstrates that he is an ordinary guy with the same ups and downs as everyone else, then it's easier for people in the church to be authentic. In sermons, I deal openly — after getting permission — with issues of our marriage and parenting, our challenges and struggles, and my weaknesses, mistakes, and failures. It's a healthy thing that many pastors and church planters preach more honestly and openly today, as opposed to the more formal and less transparent way people delivered sermons a generation ago.

There used to be an unspoken "Never let 'em see you sweat" mentality. Some pastors presented themselves as if they had personally overcome sin forever. But listen to Paul's authenticity as he writes a letter to a new church: "I was shown mercy so that in me, *the worst of sinners*, Christ Jesus might display his immense patience as an example for those who would believe in him and receive eternal life" (1 Tim. 1:16, emphasis added).

You'd be amazed at how many people still believe, no matter how many times we explain it, that they're not worthy of God's forgiveness. If we, the leaders, come across as stainless saints, we may make God seem farther away. People need Christian leaders whose imperfections are not hidden, leaders who testify to what the love and forgiveness of Christ can accomplish. If we want to build authentic believers, we must be willing to be models of authenticity.

> The main thing for me is preaching the gospel to myself much more than to the church.
>
> I must remind myself daily that I am a sinner in desperate need of a Savior.
>
> I must remind myself that I need the gospel as much as, or more than, the people in my church.
>
> I must remind myself that though my sin is great, my Savior is greater.
>
> This keeps me grounded. This keeps me real. This keeps me authentic.
>
> — Darrin (and Amie) Patrick, pastor of The Journey, St. Louis, MO, and vice president of Acts 29 Church Planting Network

Authentic Ministry

Finally, if you want to remain authentic as a leader, pursue an authentic ministry. Go after the authentic Jesus. Minister to authentic needs. When we boil it all down — this whole exploding movement of church planting — it's all about taking Jesus to people and being Jesus to people. It's really rather simple, isn't it?

As church planters, we spend a great deal of time thinking about demographics, worship styles, strategies, and so on. But ultimately it's about souls. It's about people and what's inside them. Jesus came into communities helping, healing, offering authentic hope and love. In his time, nobody else offered real hope. Nobody else knew how to really love. It's the same way now, the same way in every culture. What we have to offer is so simple, so basic, and people are so starving for it, so desperate for us to stop talking about it and start doing it.

Sometimes we make this thing more complicated than it really is.

Jud Wilhite, of Central Christian Church in Las Vegas, says that if you reach out to the broken people, you'll always have an audience. Being authentic means admitting that we are *all* broken people—that the church isn't a museum for the best and the brightest but a hospital where we can all get help for wounds no one else in the world can heal. Authenticity is modeled by Jesus, who lived a perfect life yet refused to remain on a pedestal. He came down off it to show us what love is.

> In your relationships with one another, have the same mindset as Christ Jesus: Who, being in very nature God, did not consider equality with God something to be used to his own advantage; rather, he made himself nothing by taking the very nature of a servant, being made in human likeness. And being found in appearance as a man, he humbled himself by becoming obedient to death—even death on a cross!
>
> —PHILIPPIANS 2:5–8

Before Jesus came, people could only *hear* about God and what he was like. There was no way they could *see* it. Jesus came, lived among us, and said, *"This* is what God is like. *This* is how much he loves you all." He said it as he embraced lepers, dined with outcasts, and forgave his own murderers. This is exactly what authentic church planting is supposed to be. We go where the people are, just as Jesus did. We go after the broken people, not the beautiful ones. We go into their homes, their schools, their baseball diamonds.

Just as it was two thousand years ago, people believe there is no God, at least no God who cares about what happens in the world. They don't know much about the church, but they know there's been some hypocrisy. They know there have been some judgmental religious people. There has been moral failure. Most of all, there has been a whole lot of apathy toward them, the hurting ones, and their plight. These people don't want to see anything that isn't authentic. They want you to show them the real thing — or turn around and go home.

So you say, *"This* is what God is like. *This* is how much he loves you all." And then, once you've said it, you have to back it up. You have to be authentic. That means getting down into the dust and washing some dirty feet, bandaging some really messy wounds, drying some tears that keep coming and coming. You need to be sure you understand that this is what your calling is all about. It's

Throughout my (Linda's) twenty-five years of marriage and full-time ministry, I have never put pressure on myself to perform as a "pastor's wife," meet the expectations (often unrealistic) of me, or otherwise plant or grow the church. Sure, I have always worked faithfully and sacrificially alongside my husband, Mark. But I recognized long ago that any real or perceived responsibilities of ministry must flow first and foremost from an authentic, personal relationship with Jesus Christ. This is a relationship that I cultivate intentionally through Bible reading, journaling, and prayer, on a daily basis. As a woman, wife, and ministry leader, I find that it is this relationship that keeps me growing, grounded, secure, and significant, in ways not even my husband can deliver.

At the end of the day, my authenticity is found in who I am, not what I do. It is defined by a vision of the woman I want to be when I'm eighty years old, not by how big I hope our church is

messy and uncomfortable at times, but it's 100 percent genuine gospel, and it's the only thing in the world that God wants.

If your church plant is established, be certain you're working hard to create a culture of caring in your church. If you're just beginning your plant, start with caring from the get-go. As you reach people, make sure they know that with your church, it's all about service. Find the needs and minister. Then, as you send out people to do that, just as Jesus sent out his disciples, people will experience the life of the church as it is meant to be — not a country club, not an entrepreneurial experiment or a marketing event. They'll experience what it means for Jesus to walk in this world again. And just as it happened in Judea, the crowds will come flocking to see and experience Jesus in the midst of their community.

in five years or by the latest ministry trends. I remain authentic because of my authentic love for Jesus.

For my (Mark's) part, authenticity flows from a very real and sometimes painful understanding of my own humanity. I planted a church not because I was confident but because I was called; not because I'm worthy of being followed but because I'm still learning to follow; not because I am uniquely qualified but because I've been uniquely forgiven by a God in heaven who delights to use me in spite of myself. Aware of such things, I find the freedom to be myself, that is, to measure myself not by the standards of others but by the standards of God — obedience, faith, courage, and sacrifice. Like Linda, I live not to please others but to one day hear him say, "Well done, good and faithful servant." This, as they say, keeps it real for me; it can for you as well.

— Mark and Linda DeYmaz,
Mosaic Church, Little Rock, AK

Questions to Think About

1. How Comfortable Are You in the Gifts and Abilities You Already Have?

It's easy to model ourselves after successful names in our field. We forget that the Holy Spirit is available to us to the same extent he is available to the big names of ministry. We also forget that we have the precise gifts we need to do the job God wants us to do. The other gifts will come through people around us and people we reach.

Be certain you know exactly what makes you tick. Understand your spiritual gifts and human talents, but also know where the gaps are, where you need other people who are accomplished and ready to join forces and serve God with you.

2. Do You Understand Where You Are Most Vulnerable to Temptation?

If you were Satan, where would you base your strategy? None of us like to reflect on where we're weak, but to ignore our points of weakness is to invite attack. Think about your personality, your passions, and where you've stumbled in the past. What are you doing to shore up your defenses in order to deal with these vulnerabilities? What kinds of accountability systems can you build into your ministry?

3. Are You Susceptible to the Rock Star Trap?

Pride is the most dangerous hook of all for so many leaders. The mark of the greatest Christian leaders, however, is humility based in the character of Christ.

How will you control the ego issue in your church-planting experience? What will you do to create an environment in which the pastor is not put on a pedestal?

4. Are You Creating a Culture of Caring?

Authentic ministry is about reaching out to the broken people. How is that happening in your church plant? How often do you speak on the topics of ministry and service? How many programs are built on helping people rather than entertaining them? How do you, as a leader, model authentic ministry?

CHAPTER 10

WHY IS SPIRITUAL VITALITY SO IMPORTANT?

Don't Let Your Inner Fire Go Out

At the beginning, we had our days of struggle. Our crisis had to be weathered, and then we suddenly felt like a genuine church, a congregation that was rooted and here to stay. As we moved into 1998 and passed the two hundred mark in weekly attendance, we knew God was up to something. Amy and I, along with the three couples working with us, poured ourselves body, soul, and spirit into the growth and nurture of that church.

I traveled overseas twice for trips of eight and ten days — once to Jamaica, once to Israel. In June, our second child, Zachary, was born, and we were making that transition from one little one to a much trickier *two*. Our church did the same thing in September — it went from one Sunday service to a more challenging two. Adding services brings more opportunity for growth. Soon we were bringing in three hundred each Sunday and barely squeezing by financially. Our church was one year old, and that year had been amazing, unpredictable, emotionally charged, exhausting.

One morning I rose from bed and took a good look at myself in the mirror. I rubbed my eyes, cleared my vision, and the image didn't improve. I had gained a little weight. I looked and felt tired. Since childhood and all through college, I'd been an athlete and prided myself on being in shape. Lately I had been consuming books about strategy and planning and logistics. I'd become so busy doing the work of God that I found myself neglecting the work God wanted to do inside me.

I remembered the days of calm before the storm. It was a good thing I had drawn close to the Lord then. But intimacy with God isn't a contractual arrangement. It's a relationship that must be maintained. I had been exerting all my energies to serve God, but I found myself denying him the thing he wanted first from me: my time, my heart, my devotion.

I can remember driving home from church exhilarated and excited over the growth and life change taking place. And I would look over at Amy, and there were tears running down her face. She was thrilled too — but exhausted. I was seeing the blessings firsthand. She was hearing about them secondhand, in the car; she was in survival mode. How long would she remain in the preschool ministry without ever being free to attend a service? That became a guiding question for me. Along with other needs, I needed answers from God.

At the end of 1998, I made a commitment before him that I was going to get my life — body, mind, and spirit — back into balance. Otherwise I knew I couldn't lead a church. We lead from the overflow of what's happening inside us, and in our lives the needle was sitting on empty. This was the point when I began the forty-day fast and created the fourteen-point prayer list that led to so much breakthrough for our church — and of course for my hungry spirit. Sometime later I met with Andy Stanley and came to a healthier understanding about taking care of my marriage and home. Amy and I discussed some changes we knew we'd need to make in the way we lived.

At the same time, I had a mentor named Doug Randlett. During my early days of ministry, he had been a guiding light for me. Doug had counseled me during the time that Amy and I were dating. He and his wife, Jane, were our dear friends. During the summer of 2000, when I visited with him, he was the director of ministries at Christ Fellowship Church in Palm Beach Gardens, Florida. One day, as he and I had breakfast together, he began to talk with me about the whole span of my career — the long haul. I was living so much in the present moment, and I was so consumed with the business of leadership, that I really hadn't stopped to consider things from that perspective. Younger people seldom do. Through our twenties and into our thirties, we're at our peak of energy and strength. We know it won't always be that way, but we just don't have time to confront the implications of the pace we're setting. As young adults, we're built for speed, and we enjoy going hard.

Doug made me confront the idea of the marathon. "It sounds like you've got a great thing going," he said. "But if you're going to sustain what you're doing, you'll have to be very intentional about the way you handle your ministry, your marriage, and your

Everything God desires to do *through* my life he will accomplish out of the overflow of what he is doing *in* my life. That simple reality has been the driving passion for Kristie and me for twenty years of marriage and ministry. The single most important aspect of marriage and ministry is one's personal love relationship with Jesus Christ. It is the wellspring of personal holiness and the platform through which God works through our lives for his glory and the expansion of his kingdom. As husband/wife, parent, church planter, or pastor, the number one pursuit is intimacy with Christ. We must always remember that ministry is not the primary call on our lives. The primary call is intimacy with God, and ministry is what he does out of the overflow of intimacy.

— Vance and Kristie Pitman,
Hope Church, Las Vegas, NV

family." It comes back to Jesus's parable about building a tower: You'd better have a plan. You'd better count the cost.

"I want to give you four checkpoints," Doug said. "These are things God has shared with me over the years, checkpoints for spiritual vitality." We talked about there being no easy formulas for knowing and serving God. Walking with God cannot be broken down into a checklist. Only a living relationship will do. But we can use touchstones, or markers, to help us reflect on whether we're taking good enough care of ourselves to make the long journey. Amy used to run cross-country, and she talks about how markers along a course would help her know how far along she was, whether she was on the course, and whether she was pacing herself correctly.

I have used Doug's markers for my marathon. I've added three more to make a total of seven, all beginning with *H*, simply to help me remember them. I go through them often, asking myself whether I'm on track with each one in my life and leadership. I hope these H Factors can be helpful to your own journey.

Healthiness

We have to speak of health holistically: physically, spiritually, and emotionally. Jesus said that the greatest commandment, Priority One, is this: "Love the Lord your God with all your heart and with all your soul and with all your strength and with all your mind" (Luke 10:27). Since a chain is only as strong as its weakest link, I must care for body, mind, and soul alike. Each of them has a profound effect on the others, so I can't starve any of the three.

The great thing is that they all enhance one another. For example, I know that I need to be in an exercise regimen at all times. Perspiration releases endorphins, clearing my head and helping me emotionally by relieving stress. I'm tightly wired, and exercising is good for the machine that is God's amazing creation, the human body. Running, working out, and cycling are good maintenance measures for me.

Exercise is also great for the spirit. I use that time as a worship experience. As my body takes over, that leaves my mind open for God to speak. So a workout experience is good for everything that is me — mentally, physically, spiritually, and emotionally. Amy is my partner in holding me accountable to this regimen. She has a vitality plan of her own, and we encourage each other. I keep in mind the truth of 1 Corinthians 3:16, that I'm a temple of God in which his Spirit comes to dwell. That's a high honor. If God is coming to stay, then I don't want to give him a shabby guest room. I want it to be the best possible temple, sturdy and strong, worthy of his presence.

Being spiritually healthy is about sharpening the spiritual disciplines. Like everyone else, I can become bored, so I need to be creative and find new ways to approach God, new ways to spend time with him. Isn't that what we do when a marriage becomes stale? We do the little things to bring adventure and newness to it. A relationship with God is the same way. Everyone has something that works best for them, and for me it's journaling. I use my Bible, my journal, and my worship music to help me enter God's presence.

If I can make it to a beach a couple times per year, that can be an intense spiritual experience for me. I look across the depth of the ocean, hear its power, think about its constancy over thousands of years, and I feel the presence of God. Amy and I need to escape to some beach somewhere and see that regularly, so our souls are reminded of God's greatness.

Fasting is one more approach I've used to experience God in a new way. Since body, mind, and spirit are all intertwined, emptying my body helps me to empty my spirit and have a more intense and intimate encounter with God.

Emotional health is an elusive thing. Men in particular can

be very disconnected to the state of their feelings. They can go lengthy periods of time walking that long, downhill slope toward depression, a slope so gradual that they don't realize where they're heading. Sometimes it's people around them, people who love them the most, who have to wake them up and say, "Listen to me. You're not happy. I can see it even if you can't. We have to do something about it."

Troubled emotions, whether depression, intense anxiety, or something else, cannot simply be stuffed into some attic closet of the mind. We have to deal with our feelings. When you find yourself struggling emotionally, don't be afraid to get help. It's not a referendum on your spiritual maturity. Some of the greatest Christians in our history, leaders such as Charles Spurgeon, dealt with severe depression. Some of our great leaders today have spoken out during the last few years about the blessing of counseling in their lives. We're all human.

My great crisis moment came when I lost my dad in a rafting accident. It wiped me out emotionally, devastated me. For a number of months between 2004 and 2005, I was in an emotional fog. I kept working, preparing sermons, leading our staff, supervising the construction of a building, and being there for my family. But there was a lot to deal with — not only for me, but also for my mother and my thirteen-year-old brother, who were also devastated.

I realized there was no way I could handle everything that was on my shoulders. God loves us, he wants to care for us in every way, and he gave us people with special gifts to walk us through those dark valleys. I saw that I had to be open, admit I was in over my head, and get some assistance. Even if you're emotionally strong right now, you need a plan for the time when you may not be. You need to be intentional about every area of your health — body, mind, and spirit.

Humility

"Humble yourselves, therefore, under God's mighty hand, that he may lift you up in due time" (1 Peter 5:6). We mentioned in the last chapter that pride is an enormous stumbling block for pastors and planters. You could say that this is true for nearly everyone else too.

Pride is the root of sin, the establishment of an idol — self — above the one true God. Charles Stanley has said that pride is the one sin that says to God, "I don't need you." Its lure is so pervasive, so constant, that we need to take Peter's advice and pursue true humility on a daily basis. Peter says to do this in God's strength, because we'll never be capable of it on our own. How? Through keeping in step with the Spirit of God, who lives within us and gives us that daily reality check to help us remember that without his strength, we are nothing.

I have a strong personality as a leader. I'm competitive and driven toward making things happen. These are assets to leadership, until they cross that fine line and become arrogance. So with God's help, I have to guard that line vigilantly. I've seen what happens when people don't guard the line. I've been in rooms filled with church leaders who are jockeying for position, telling their success stories, one-upping each other; the pride level in those rooms is almost toxic.

There's a reason why Jesus devoted so much of his teaching to the servant mentality. He walked along the road and overheard his disciples' arguments. It was the same jockeying for position, the same battle for the best seat at the Lord's table. "Sitting down, Jesus called the Twelve and said, 'Anyone who wants to be first must be the very last, and the servant of all'" (Mark 9:35). I imagine that put an end to the dispute.

Humility in leadership is the key to having God's hand on your life. "God opposes the proud but shows favor to the humble"

(James 4:6). In my mind, there is an image of the God of the universe holding up his hand, opposing me because of my pride. That idea is more than I can handle. The quickest way for it to happen is for me to become prideful and self-centered.

God is jealous over his glory. He says, "I am the LORD; that is my name! I will not yield my glory to another or my praise to idols" (Isa. 42:8). There's a reason why the first commandment he gave to Moses stipulated that there could be *no other gods*. Almost anything can be a god, from pride to pleasure to power to possessions, but pride is the one that steals into the throne room the most elusively.

I've already written about my Saddleback experience, when I internalized the idea that it's not about me. I'm sure we all give lip service to that concept. I've yet to hear a pastor walk onstage and say, "You know what? It *is* all about me!" But really taking hold of that idea seriously is a liberating thing because at the end of the day, if it's about me, then it's not about much. If it's about me, then I'm on the spot. I have to carry that burden. I have to find some way of measuring up to all of this being about something as not-ready-for-prime-time as *me*.

Of course I can't measure up. If it's about me, it fails, because I'm going to let everyone down. Only God is worthy of holding that distinction. I need to understand this every day, to die to self one more time and be reminded that he is all in all, and I am only his vessel. That's *freeing*. That takes the pressure off my shoulders and allows me to serve him with joy and energy. He gives grace to the humble, and I need that grace every day.

If I can stay humble, that's a difference maker. It means I can pull for other pastors to succeed, and really mean it, because we're now working for the same King instead of competing kingdoms. Humility allows me to see the big picture, to be part of the great expanse of God's kingdom, rather than experience the suffocation of caring only about what happens within our own little walls.

Humility is powerful, but it takes a plan. What is your everyday plan for combating sinful pride and embracing humility?

Home

When we accepted the invitation to write this book, one of the most urgent topics we wanted to discuss was how important it is for church planters to protect their homes. We saw too many planters taking damage to their marriages and their parenting because of the demands of building a church.

We live in such a highly competitive world today that there is an unwritten, unacknowledged message that if you want to be successful, you'd better place your work before all else. You would think that the Christian world, as family oriented and home affirming as it is, would champion the sanctity of the family and advocate the need to keep it healthy and strong. But many church staffs fall into the cultural delusion of career success as the greatest value; we simply spiritualize the worldly concept of success. And we assume that if we've accepted a call to build God's kingdom, he will take care of all the surrounding stuff. We can throw ourselves totally into the perspiration of ministry as God ensures that our spouses and children are okay.

But in our family chapter, we showed how this is the worst kind of deception. God expects us to have the right priorities, and the home must come before church work—or everything else will fall apart in time. Therefore we need to be aware that Satan is out to take down our homes, knowing it's the surest way to destroy our ministries. If my marriage is in turmoil and my children are troubled, I won't be much good for the church I'm serving. Ultimately, it comes down to a question of priorities—and having a deliberate plan for taking care of my home. If you're a planter, you need to decide the scope of your responsibilities. If you have your hand in everything, you need to ask God to bring people alongside you to take on some of those roles and become specialists.

From the very beginning, you need to have a good idea of what it is that you do best. When God has brought the full team together someday, and you have all the specialists in place, what will you be left doing? What is your own key contribution? The better and the sooner and the more specifically you can answer that question, the fewer bags you'll be left holding. People will recognize what you're called to do, and they'll help by doing everything else. At all times, from the very beginning, family goes at the very top of the list. If you are married, that's the most important job God has given you. If you have children, that's your second-most-important job.

Even if a volunteer or staff member won't do some particular task exactly the way you like it done, exactly as you have done it, you still must be willing to let them do it, or even fail at times. Establish what your values are, what your vision is, and then turn people loose to serve.

I can remember the days of doing everything. But after fifteen years as pastor at West Ridge, I have a clear idea of what I'm supposed to be doing. Here are my roles, in no particular order:

- Shepherding and pastoring
- Teaching
- Praying for our people and being a champion of our prayer ministries
- Leading and casting vision
- Planting churches (the LAUNCH Church Planting Network)
- Bringing churches together in Atlanta (Engage Atlanta) for community transformation

It has taken me fifteen years to fine-tune that list. What would your list look like?

In the family chapter, Amy and I have discussed some of the

values that help us place our family at the top of our priority list. I have a very clear plan for strengthening our home. What's your plan?

Happiness

We spend a lot of time chasing an elusive goal. The planter never comes home at night, kisses his wife at the door, and says, "We accomplished everything possible for the eternal glory of God today. We defeated the work of Satan at every single turn. Every need among our people was ministered to, and every lost person we encountered was saved. What's on TV?"

We're driven to succeed, to produce, to grow things, and to get tangible results within a spiritual context where so many things are intangible. It can be very difficult to attain simple content-ment in the moment — to know that though whatever we're build-ing will always remain a work in progress, we're right where God wants us to be. I try to remember several important truths about happiness.

First, happiness is a matter of *assurance* that God is in con-trol. I have to let go and let God determine how things are going to shake out. I try to claim the following passage and ground my heart in the truth of it.

> "Yours, LORD, is the greatness and the power and the glory and the majesty and the splendor, for everything in heaven and earth is yours. Yours, LORD, is the kingdom; you are exalted as head over all. Wealth and honor come from you; you are the ruler of all things. In your hands are strength and power to exalt and give strength to all."
>
> —1 CHRONICLES 29:11–12

At some point I need to trust in the sovereignty of God. It's all in his hands. If I give my best and work in the best light I have from him, I should be able to be content as I entrust my work to his perfect plan and power.

Second, happiness is really a matter of *joy*, its ultimate source, and I have to remember where joy comes from. People spend a lot of time, effort, and passion trying to find joy in life. But I can't produce it, and neither can anyone else. Joy is a fruit of the Spirit (Gal. 5:22–23). Only the Holy Spirit can bring genuine joy into my life. What I can do, however, is to make the choice to be filled with the Spirit and to allow him to bring the joy that comes through the Spirit-filled life. Therefore I find happiness by stepping back and letting Christ be the Lord of my heart and mind, my thoughts and my ambitions, my past and my future.

Third, happiness is a matter of *focus*. I've heard Tom Holladay, a teaching pastor at Saddleback Church, give the following illustration. Imagine your family drives for days to reach the Grand Canyon on a vacation. As you arrive, you pull out the lawn chairs, find a nice spot, and settle down to take in the glorious view of God's creation. Suddenly the beautiful sounds of nature are broken by the grinding of a diesel engine as a large Winnebago pulls up — right in your line of vision. Now all you can see is that great box on wheels.

You then have a choice. You can remain in your chair with an eyeful of Winnebago and become more and more resentful. *Or* you can get up, move your lawn chairs, and pick up where you left off, enjoying the scenery. You just have to refocus your view. Move your chair! Too many people focus on the obstructions rather than the awesome grandeur of the Lord, which we can always see; it's just a question of focus.

Fourth, happiness is a matter of Jesus being enough. I ask myself nearly every day, *What if all this were taken away?* Would Jesus be enough? What if God stripped my life of all the trappings, the church culture, the organizations, the structures, and the system of everything; would Jesus be enough? I've asked plant-ers this question and heard them honestly answer, "No." I believe that a lot of people would *honestly* have to give that answer. Is Jesus enough for you, or are you after something else all the time? I truly believe that the way you answer that question will determine how much happiness you can experience in ministry.

How do you maintain spiritual vitality while planting a church?

Staying spiritually sharp will simply be a struggle; Satan will see to it. Expect it. Spiritual vitality will not come to you from the church you're planting. Don't look to the church or your team to keep you close to God; it won't and neither will they. If anything, leading a church plant will mostly drain spiritual energy from you. If you're going to stay in step with the One who called you and for whom you're planting this church, you must become ruthlessly intentional about it. Discover how you most naturally connect with God personally in ways that are not necessarily linked to the church, and make those experiences a priority. Whether it's a long walk through the woods, running, hiking, fishing, reading, solitude, painting, music, or something else, find what best pro-pels your heart toward his.

Staying spiritually sharp will also require sharpening. Listen to the voices of those who've gone before you. Seek out men and women of God who've "been there" and lived to tell you about it. Every leader needs to be led. Every teacher needs to be taught. Every pastor still needs one. Allow God to fill your spiritual tank with the wisdom and insight of those who are a few steps ahead of you on the journey. They've been there to help you get there. That's part of God's assignment for them and a gift of God's grace to your heart and leadership.

— Jonathan and Donna Robbins,
The Summit Church, Winston Salem, NC

Holiness

There are various studies now that all paint a frightening picture of great numbers of pastors and Christian leaders hooked on pornography. Rick Warren surveyed six thousand pastors, and 30 percent admitted to viewing Internet porn during the most recent thirty days. Patrick Means's book *Men's Secret Wars** suggests that 64 percent of all evangelical leaders admit to struggling with some form of sexual addiction. It's time we stop thinking of this as a problem of "the world" and admit that it's a problem within the church, up to and including the level of leadership.

Pornography isn't the only problem. Amy and I have counseled several church planters who have fallen into affairs. We've sat in the living room with a couple as the husband confessed to his wife that he'd been physically or emotionally involved with another woman. It's one of the most difficult tasks Amy and I have faced as we've worked with church planters. We've seen the irreparable damage done to the children, and the fallout within the pastor's church. So much hard work, so much godly work, is lost. It takes years to rebuild a church's image in a community after a public moral failure.

So much is at stake in whether we choose to live in a manner worthy of our calling. Paul writes, "Dear friends, let us purify ourselves from everything that contaminates body and spirit, perfecting holiness out of reverence for God" (2 Cor. 7:1). To be holy is to be set apart for a purpose. If you set apart a special suit, you keep it spotless and clean for special occasions. As church planters, we want our lives to be pure. Yet we're busy working in the world. We can't flee to a monastery in the desert, because God wants us to be fishers of men. Somehow we must be in the world yet remain clean from its impurities. Only in the power of God is that possible.

---

*Grand Rapids: Revell, 2006.

I think about my moment in the Georgia Dome, when God was first calling us, and he put Joshua 3:5 on my heart: "Consecrate yourselves, for tomorrow the LORD will do amazing things among you." When a life is consecrated, it is fully devoted to God's service. You see yourself as a temple of the Holy Spirit, and there are certain things that aren't permitted in the temple.

We need to take stock of our attitudes, our passions, and our desires and lay them before God. We are weak, while the pull of worldliness is incredibly powerful today. However, the New Testament tells us that Christ "has become for us wisdom from God — that is, our righteousness, holiness and redemption" (1 Cor. 1:30). This is a significant idea. Jesus *himself* is my holiness. He has already cleansed me in God's sight, already purified me so that I can come before God. Therefore I need to yield myself before him. He knows best; his purposes are best. And the closer I draw to him, the more clearly I'll see the foolishness of the world's temptations.

I take care to put guardrails around my life, and I've already discussed them in another chapter — declining to counsel women unless my wife is in the room, for example; having the Internet safely filtered at home and at the office; declining, when possible, to travel alone. These are rules I've built into my life for my own protection. I guard my choices constantly, and I talk to my boys about the wisdom of that. The choices we make in life, step by step, day by day, determine our future.

Life is too short, and the stakes are too high, for wasting ourselves on secret sin, which of course usually makes itself public sooner or later. We need to focus on Christ, focus on the blessings he has given us through our family and through our calling, and then ask God to show us temptation and sin for what they really are. We can't afford to trade gold for garbage. If you're going to live a life of purity and holiness, you'll need a plan. Have you devised it?

Honesty

In our twenties, we think we know everything. In our thirties, we think we can do everything. In our forties, we take a deep breath and a fresher, wiser look at reality. We realize life is short, we are limited, and the world frankly doesn't care whether we succeed or fail. By that time, we're seeing some of our friends fail in business and in their families. The naiveté has worn off. It's time to take stock, time to figure out how to make the best use of the second half of life.

I went through that process at the age of forty. In a way, it was freeing to get past thinking I could do everything and be all things to all people. If I was going to accomplish any worthy goals in life, I would need to be much more deliberate. I'd need to know what I could do well and what I could not.

My verse for honesty is, "By the grace given me I say to every one of you: Do not think of yourself more highly than you ought, but rather think of yourself with sober judgment, in accordance with the faith God has distributed to each of you" (Rom. 12:3). *Sober judgment.* That's a pretty good description of what life gives us in exchange for our years. We're able to look at ourselves with clear-eyed focus, see who we really are, and also be transparent so that others can see who we really are.

Are you going to make truth and authenticity a priority in your spiritual life? What's your plan for doing so?

Hunger

Jesus speaks of those "who hunger and thirst for righteousness." And what is his promise? "They will be filled" (Matt. 5:6). I felt that hunger during our first summer in Atlanta, just prior to our launching West Ridge. My heart was desperate for God. We had been filled in Lynchburg; we had full lives. To pursue the life of church planting, we gave up certain things, certain comforts. We started with basically nothing—low finances, no distractions, few relationships in the Atlanta area. We wanted to cast ourselves upon the resources of God and God alone, and the intimacy with him during that time was unforgettable. We wanted to be filled. Never had we felt so much in tune with his Spirit.

Then West Ridge began. I was burning the candle at both ends, reading every book available on church planting and leadership, knocking on doors, thinking and planning. The faster our church grew, the emptier my tank seemed to be. I was beginning to run dry. That's when I came to the decision to begin my forty-day fast, to pull body, mind, and spirit back together, and particularly to draw closer to God again. It is very possible to attempt to do the work of God in the power of the flesh, rather than drawing on divine resources.

The time of fasting drew me closer to God in prayer. He reminded me why I'd left Virginia in the first place. It wasn't about building an organization; it was about finding where God was working and joining him there. I had wanted to see God do amazing things, mighty things. I wanted to see lives changed forever as I let him work through me and through our team. I'd come to work *with God*—but sometimes it felt like I was just working.

The Bible teaches that there's a part of us called "the flesh" that is opposed to the spirit. Many Christians don't understand that the flesh never completely dies—not during this earthly life. This is why we can still have rough days, still give in to sinful desires, even though we've been saved and have Christ living in us. The old self lives on.

In the movies, there are monsters that won't die. The hero picks up his rifle and blows the creature away, over and over, but the thing just gets up and keeps coming. The flesh—the old version of you—is like that. We have to keep crucifying it every single day, because living in the flesh robs us of the experience of living in God's power. It substitutes our limited, flawed resources for the infinite power of God's Spirit. And it destroys our hunger to know God intimately.

This is why we have the concept of revival in our faith. We are so prone to wander, so prone to leave the path and go back to doing things the old way, the defeated way. We need wake-up calls from time to time so we can ask ourselves, "Am I living under my own power, or am I depending totally upon God? Am I hungry for his Word and to hear his voice each day, or have I let other things push God's things away?"

I think of a man out in the harbor, sitting in a boat. He is bending to the oar, rowing for all he's worth, and barely getting anywhere. As he stops to wipe away the sweat, another boat comes alongside him. Its pilot calls out, "Hey there, friend! It must be your first time in that boat!"

The rower says it's true, and the visitor climbs into his boat and shows him that there is a mast with a mainsail. He shows him how to raise the great sail and adjust it. Suddenly a strong wind puffs out the white sheet, the boat lurches in the water, and the man puts down his oar and simply begins to steer, with a tremendous grin on his face. "This is wonderful!" he says. "Why didn't anyone ever tell me I could travel in such style?"

I think there are a lot of people who don't understand the difference between living by the power of the Holy Spirit, with the wind at your back, and trying to be a Christian through human exertion. When you're hungry for God, and nothing but God, his Spirit comes alongside you, fills you, propels you across the sea of life. Then your journey becomes a glorious voyage instead of a sentence of hard labor. Jesus says, "Take my yoke upon you and learn from me, for I am gentle and humble in heart, and you will find rest for your souls. For my yoke is easy and my burden is light" (Matt. 11:29–30).

If you don't find that rest for your soul, you'll be forever weary until you burn out entirely. If you don't consume the Bread of Life, you'll be hungry forever, for things that never fill your soul. Are you hungry for God? Desperate to hear his voice? "You will find him if you seek him with all your heart and with all your soul" (Deut. 4:29). That's a promise. Come to the table with a great appetite. You just have to be hungry.

Questions to Think About

What is your plan for each of these H Factors? Write it down. Put it into action.

- Healthiness
- Humility
- Home
- Happiness
- Holiness
- Honesty
- Hunger

CHAPTER 11

HOW CAN YOU THRIVE IN THE JOURNEY?

Are We Having Fun Yet?

They call it the Roller Coaster Capital of the World: Cedar Point, in Sandusky, Ohio. It has more rides than any other park, including four roller coasters taller than two hundred feet. A couple of years ago we decided to make it a family pilgrimage. We thought we knew the park; at least, we had memories of it from growing up. But this was a whole new world: 364 acres of color and food and noise and screaming and chaos.

We walked in with our boys, my mom, and some extended family from Michigan and took a good look around us. Amy and I wondered whether this was something we were going to enjoy or something we were merely going to survive. I remembered the thrill of riding the Blue Streak, the Corkscrew, and Gemini years ago. Those rides would be kiddie stuff now, because there was the Wicked Twister. There was Millennium Force. And there was something called the Top Thrill Dragster. I wasn't really sure I wanted to strap into something that sounded like a high-tech assault weapon! I didn't know if I wanted to be taken 420 feet into the air, then whipped around at 120 miles per hour.

At the gate, they handed us this great, colorful "fun map," a detailed overhead picture of every ride in the park and all the paths leading every which way, looking vaguely like intestines — fairly appropriate for something that we *knew* was about to mess with our stomachs. This place seemed to cover several zip codes. Moses and the Israelites might have wandered for forty years here. It was intimidating. But we took a minute and simply looked around at the throngs flowing along the pathways in all directions. *This is pretty ingenious*, I thought. *This park is really doable for anybody; you just have to know what's right for you and have a plan.*

After all, there was no law that said you had to board the most vicious ride in the place. There were a few "milder" coasters you could substitute. You could see grandparents and their very young grandchildren riding the old-school Ferris wheels or merry-go-rounds — or just sitting in the food court, hanging out and taking in the ambience. You could sit on one of the benches and go over that fun map with the family, then make your plan — figure out who wants to go where, when to meet up again, that kind of thing. As it worked out, everyone in our group had a phenomenal time, from the oldest to the youngest. Everything we had loved about the park was still there, but there was so much more. We just had to understand what was there and have a plan so we could thrive rather than merely survive.

I submit to you that the scenario I've laid out suggests the right strategy for a career of planting and building a church. If I were to sit down and create a great, foldable map of the history of West Ridge Church, it might resemble Cedar Point, at least a little. It would be very colorful. There would be lots of scary attractions and wild events. There would be people everywhere, sometimes laughing, sometimes crying, sometimes sick or lost. I would look down at the map and say, "How could I ever cover all this territory in one lifetime?"

I'm not sure I'd have wanted to see that map in advance. One of the magnificent graces of God is that most of the time, he allows us to only see in a mirror dimly. He doesn't give us the fun map of a life of ministry. We're usually better off not knowing exactly what's around the next bend.

Planting a church isn't always a day in the park, but I think it's thrilling, wonderful, and makes your typical amusement park seem pretty dull in comparison. It takes you high in the sky, whips you around at supersonic speed, and leaves you all but breathless. I'm thankful for the journey we've made—even the roller-coaster moments, the crazy pace, and the price of admission. I know this is a journey worth making, but one we shouldn't have to settle for surviving. It ought to be fun. It ought to be joyful. If you have the wisdom to be proactive, you can create a plan that will enable you to thrive along the journey. I'd like to ask you several questions to help you create your plan.

Can You Be Intentional about This Journey?

I've suggested that certain personality types are attracted to church planting. If we did a survey, I believe that we would find that a disproportionate number of ADD/ADHD people have taken up this cause. They're drawn to excitement, to newness, to creativity and daily variety; they like amusement parks. Church planting does bring a high level of excitement. But it's a great mistake to live only in the moment, without planning ahead. Many of the church planters we've met need to be thinking in longer terms. It's true that cultural and technological changes are now coming on us so quickly that we can't set our plans in stone for the long term; there has to be a great deal of flexibility. Your vision should be solid, but your plans must be fluid. A couple of decades ago nobody could have predicted what the church—or our world— would look like today.

But we do have to realize that church planting is a journey. It's not just about today; it's about tomorrow and next year and the next decade. This raises questions we all have to confront. Considering what you're doing right now, could you do it ten years from now? Twenty? Can you sustain the lifestyle and maintain the pace you're setting right now? Also, we've talked about isolating our best gifts, the ones we intend to keep using as others come along to take on complementary tasks. What's your plan for recruitment? For delegation? If you've planted a church in the last couple years, you also need a plan for growth. Where can you go once you've outgrown the cafeteria or theater or community center? What are your plans for buying and developing land? Do you have skilled people monitoring real estate values in your area?

There are many more issues to consider, of course. The Bible makes three key points about our plans. First, it's wise to be organized and to have a plan dedicated to God's glory: "Commit to the LORD whatever you do, and he will establish your plans" (Prov. 16:3). I find this to be such a reassuring promise, because I know that my plans aren't perfect but I can trust my heart to him, use the mind he gave me, and get moving. Second, God wants me to take advantage of the wisdom of others: "Plans fail for lack of counsel, but with many advisers they succeed" (Prov. 15:22). If you've read this far in our book, you know that I'm a strong believer in leaning on the wisdom of others. In various fields, I've stood on the shoulders of giants, reaping the dividends of powerful advice. Third, our God is sovereign over our plans: "In their hearts humans plan their course, but the LORD establishes their steps" (Prov. 16:9). I know I've had bad ideas before, and I'll have them again. I'm thankful that God's plan trumps whatever mess I can make. He uses all things for his purposes.

Plan ahead, plan with others, and plan in faith. You can't go wrong.

Can You Let This Be God's Journey?

Or, to put it another way: *Can you move beyond your need for approval?* A great many people planting or leading churches are approval junkies. Some pastors live their entire week for the positive feedback that comes after the sermon. As a matter of fact, they walk off the stage and go directly to those friends who are most likely to give them that positive feedback.

None of us have motives that are 100 percent pure. God is graciously willing to use us despite our rough edges and our insecurities. I'm sure there are many approval seekers out there who have highly fruitful ministries. However, if you want to thrive in your journey rather than merely survive, at some point you have to let God's church be about God's glory. You'll never be satisfied if you make it about you. There will never be quite enough applause or few enough complaints.

By seeking personal honor and glory, we become consumed by inadequate goals. In Matthew 6, Jesus talks about religious leaders who do all kinds of showy things in public because of the attention it gets them. In each case, Jesus says the same thing: "They have received their reward in full" (vv. 2, 5, 16). Sad words. Why settle for such paltry rewards? Jesus tells his listeners there is something far better in store for them if they act solely to please God: "Your Father, who sees what is done in secret, will reward you" (vv. 4, 6, 18). Jesus is talking about life with the eternal, infinite God. He's talking about the full, abundant, and joyful life he came to give us, and in particular he's talking about the opportunity we have to cooperate with God in kingdom work in this life—the greatest honor anyone could ever receive.

We get the chance to shine the spotlight on the only one who is worthy of it. And yet some people use the name of God to draw attention to themselves, to bask in the reflection of his glory. The prize they chase is ultimately pale and pathetic compared with the prize of working with God to achieve godly goals.

God does honor men and women when they humble themselves and dedicate their lives to honoring him: "The LORD God is a sun and shield; the LORD bestows favor and honor; no good thing does he withhold from those whose walk is blameless"

(Ps. 84:11). Jesus says, "My Father will honor the one who serves me" (John 12:26). So we need to let the Father bring honors rather than seeking them ourselves. We don't need to ceaselessly lobby, campaign, or strain to attract attention and build a platform of self-glorification.

Amy and I never intended to write a book. That kind of hard work was not something we were eager to take on. We were approached by our friends from Exponential Network and Leadership Network, who were convinced that our story and insights could be helpful to others who were planting churches. That gave us confidence that this was something God wanted to do, something that would bring credit to him. The story of West Ridge is his story, and we're just two of the characters in his manuscript.

So the question is, can you let this journey shine fully on God? John the Baptist said, "He must become greater; I must become less" (John 3:30). Can you serve based on that plan? If so, you will thrive, because God's power comes to people who lift up his name. Self-promotion is a rat race that gets you running in circles, never finding a finish line; glorifying God is a journey whose reward is sweeter all the time.

> I've had this fear that I was inadequate, and I've allowed it to cause me to live in Pete's shadow. God has given me my own calling. I have my own set of unique gifts. I've kinda been a stranger to myself, and yet I know I have influence because I am Pete's wife. I've deadened that influence because I've been scared. For me, the hardest part of ministry is being married to the pastor. Having a community outside our church is a gift and something that I want others to have.
>
> — Brandi Wilson, Crosspointe Church, Nashville, TN, and Leading and Loving It (*www.leadingandlovingit.com*)

Can You Let This Journey Be about People?

Church planters are God's entrepreneurs. This is a golden age of creativity in the church, and that's an exciting reality. For decades, churches had a predictable look and behaved in predictable ways —the same music, the same communication styles, the same programs, year after year. Today there are new ideas, new approaches, new wineskins for a never-changing gospel that is always good news.

But we can lose God in new ideas the same way we can lose him in worn-out customs. Once we figure out what different kind of building we want to use, what new style of music we want to perform, what dynamic style of teaching we want to employ, we must come back to the truth that it's all about God providing reconciliation and redemption to people through Christ. Sometimes I'm concerned that there are church planters who are passionate about process and strategy but much less compassionate for people.

Do we think God really cares whether we have Handel or hip-hop? Whether we use video or drama? Do we think it matters to him whether we meet in a two-hundred-year-old steepled sanctuary or in a modern movie theater? These things are tools and trappings; we change them when the old tools and trappings become dusty and unattractive to the people we're trying to reach. We're not trending toward casual dress because we found it in Scripture; it's because coats and ties became one more obstacle to telling people about Jesus.

The Corinthians asked Paul whether they should eat food sacrificed to idols. Opinions varied on how God felt about that practice. At the end of 1 Corinthians 8, Paul says that the answer is, *whatever helps people hear from God more quickly.* If you're going to eat something that would offend someone and make them question your faith, don't do it—not because of the thing itself but because the issue is always *people.*

Paul is saying that God just wants us to reach and minister

to people, and the little stuff matters only as a means to that end. Some of us today are like the Corinthians who got caught up in the trappings while missing the real issue. Be as creative as you can. Use humor and style and fantastic music and multimedia and dynamic teaching to bring people in. But what will you do once you bring them in? Until then you've merely done the easy part. Now you must love people and lead them on a spiritual journey so they can become fully devoted followers of Jesus. That's prime time.

You must bind up wounds, dry tears, and listen to people who need to be heard. There will be times when you obsess all week about whether to use this illustration or that one in the sermon. And on Sunday, when you talk to people afterward, you'll find out that it wasn't about illustrations or any other sermon-related issues for the people God brought—it was about one line from a song that spoke to a need, or a stranger who walked up and offered a smile, or your personally staying afterward to chat. Your journey must be about people. God loves people.

Whenever I approach God to find out what's on his heart for West Ridge Church, through a fast or a devotional time or a personal prayer retreat, God has pretty much the same message every time. *People.* I want to say, "That again? You've got people on the brain!"

He does. All those people out there, with all their ages, all their colors, all their problems and needs—every one of them is a child of God, someone he wants brought home. Your mission in life is as simple as that. *Reach people.* Reach them and teach them to be followers of Jesus.

Don't let your church ever be about anything else. Wayne Cordeira, of New Hope Christian Fellowship in Honolulu, Hawaii, says, "We have to connect everything we do to a soul." Your church must be about taking people and making them disciples. We have said that our work is about two things: giving God glory and reaching people. Each one accomplishes the other. When we glorify God, people will come from everywhere. And whenever we reach people for Christ, God is glorified in the one way that pleases him most.

If you're going to thrive rather than simply survive, ask yourself whether you have a heart for people that reflects God's heart. I'm surprised by how many men and women in ministry have told me they really don't like people. Some of them are like Linus in the classic *Peanuts* comic strip, who said, "I love humanity. It's people I can't stand."

It's not difficult to fix that kind of heart problem. The truth is that you can't love God and not find yourself caring for his people sooner or later. He takes care of that part. Dedicate yourself to him, then go where the needs are. Get involved in helping people. Open your ears to the questions and anxieties that people bring to your church. God's Spirit will break your heart when it needs to be broken, and you'll find you're more of a people person than you thought.

Will Your Journey Be about the Future?

Here's one way to evaluate a great church: it's a *sending* church. Ask around, and you discover that young people are emerging from it to plant churches, to do mission work, to create ministries of all kinds.

Have you ever been a guest at another church, and you could just feel the electricity in the air, the vigorous sense of the Holy Spirit bonding people together and getting things going? At that church, there's a special light in people's eyes — the light of possibility, of the kingdom God wants to create. We knew when we came to Atlanta that we didn't just want to build another big box to hold a lot of people. This was going to be about truly fulfilling an Acts 1:8 mission.

God is just looking for launching pads. "The eyes of the LORD range throughout the earth to strengthen those whose hearts are fully committed to him" (2 Chron. 16:9). In great churches, you find people fully committed to him, and you find that their hearts are being strengthened for ministry. But they're not content to stay and work within the programs and structures of the home church. God comes for them; he calls them out.

If you're going to thrive on the journey of church planting, you need to see the connection between your church and eternity itself. If it's all for just right here and just today, you're going to be disappointed at times. But if you can connect the dots and see your church as part of God's tapestry, extending back to the beginning of time, forward to its end, and on to eternity, and if you can understand your church as a gathering place of multiple movements and strategies God has yet to launch, then you'll always feel that you're living on the edge of adventure.

Up to the time of my Saddleback experience in 2003, I would have told you that my calling was to the northwest Atlanta metropolitan area — and there was nothing wrong with that at all. It was a significant calling, and it's what God had for me until then. But in 2003 God pulled back the curtain for me. He showed me a much greater picture, and it was almost like being called all over again. Not only was it not about me; it wasn't just about West Ridge. It was about the larger region. And ultimately it was about the world itself. It was about tomorrow and whatever future there may be until Christ returns.

We have to change the scorecard in the way we think of and evaluate church. Is it only about numbers, about how many buildings we can put up in a career? What gets me much more excited is talking to you about the churches we've planted in our own backyard to reach our region, or the church planters we're training right now through the LAUNCH Church Planting Network, who will plant churches all over the United States, or the new churches that are being built every month in Burkina Faso, Africa.

Some churches stockpile their most talented people, keep them "inside the wall" to keep doing their thing. Wiser churches send out their best, and they know God will raise up someone else inside the wall. We commission our people to a great work. We are stewards of our human resources just as we are of our financial resources. If you're just sending money to do missions and not sending people, you're missing something extraordinary.

One of my spiritual heroes is the late Bill Bright, who founded Campus Crusade for Christ. A friend of mine worked with Dr. Bright during the great leader's final weeks of life. Dr. Bright had to breathe through a respirator. He could barely talk. He had about an hour and a half per day during which he had the strength for a conversation. But he spent that time invested in three or four world-impacting ministry projects. His body was sinking fast, but his eyes were brightly lit by the prospect of training missionaries all over the world through the Internet, getting several new books published with his latest thoughts, and developing other ideas God was still using him to launch.

I want our lives to be like that, right up to the end of the time God has given us here — thriving on the ongoing work of God rather than trying to do so on the roller coaster of human competition. If God will do so many things through one dying man, how much more could he get done through us, if only we'll be willing to be used?

Can You Let the Journey Allow for Surprises?

One aspect of a people-based, eternity-based ministry is that it will be loaded with surprises. God is like any good father who loves delighting his children. Most great leaders end up following roads they would never have set off to explore on their own initiative. Columbus had one vision, but his destiny was to discover America. Martin Luther had a passion for defending scriptural

authority; he never intended to launch the Protestant Reforma-
tion. Walt Disney was a cartoonist who ended up inventing the
theme park. Bill Bright was the leader of a college ministry, yet
he ended up (among other things) as a film entrepreneur, promoting the *Jesus* film—a movie that has been seen more than six billion times, by people all over the world, making it the most widely
viewed motion picture ever.

The work of God is like a great river that keeps pushing its way
toward the sea, always breaking into new streams and rivulets,
some of which become rivers in their own right. When God called
us to be willing to follow him out of Lynchburg years ago, he didn't
tell us initially that it was to plant a church; he simply wanted us to
be obedient. Then, when we knew he wanted us to plant a church,
that still wasn't the whole story. It's still unfolding. We can't wait
to find out what he'll do next through our ministries.

I follow the careers of great Christian leaders, and I see how
their visions evolve into wider conceptions in time. God is always
showing them something new, something he has carefully prepared them to do. If you want to thrive on this journey, be open to
godly surprises. Knowing that God may show you something life-
changing tomorrow keeps you on your toes today. It keeps cynicism
out of your life. He reveals things to us on a need-to-know basis,
never wanting to overwhelm us, never wanting us to put our energy
toward thinking about something before we're ready to tackle it.
We weren't ready to take on LAUNCH or Engage Atlanta until
the points in time when God moved us to pursue them.

Christian growth is about fruit bearing. Jesus says, "I am the
vine; you are the branches. If you remain in me and I in you, you
will bear much fruit; apart from me you can do nothing" (John
15:5). Isn't this how a fruit tree thrives? It remains connected to
its roots. As the life-giving sap flows through it, it continues to
bear fruit in season. Jesus wants us to bear much fruit. Over time,
even through seasons of pruning, the fruit we bear becomes richer,

stronger. Since we are the branches, we continue to branch out. You find this pattern in the ministries of all who abide in Christ. Some ministries become mighty orchards.

Expect surprises! They'll bring you joy and new life that will keep you young and thriving.

Can You Let the Journey Keep You Positive?

We need to acknowledge that even as great a ride as this can be, there will always be people challenging you. Success, growth, and godliness in your church — none of these are buffers against criticism. As a matter of fact, the more you ramp up your efforts, the wider your influence, the more the power of God falls upon what you do, the more opposition you will encounter.

Some of it is just people. The world is filled with unhappy people who define themselves by what they oppose. A few of them oppose anything and anyone less cynical than they are. Just notice that wherever you go, you'll see statues of achievers: explorers, philanthropists, heroes of various kinds, but you'll never see a statue of a critic. They'll be forgotten, so don't spend valuable time engaging them. I still believe in the decision we made during our living room meeting during the first crisis of our church: ignore the opposition outside the wall; face down the opposition inside, because it will cause disunity.

Opposition is spiritual warfare too. It's easy to get caught up in playing defense, rather than remaining on the offensive. You'll have to recognize unworthy distractions for what they are. At the same time, you'll need to grow an extra-thick layer of skin. It's important to acknowledge that leadership has various prices and to move on without whining about the critics and the problems. Some people who are starting new churches take on the attitude that they're just lowly church planters. They complain about the obstacles that are simply part of the process of following God's leadership.

He never promised an easy ride—just an exciting one, and one during which he will go with us and provide our deepest needs. People don't follow leaders with martyr complexes, who are glass-half-empty types. They follow positive, visionary individuals with compelling God-given messages, men and women who see stepping-stones where others see stumbling blocks.

I think every leader should make a serious self-assessment based on a simple question: "Am I a positive, energetic leader or a negative one, prone to frustration and anxiety?" If you're going to thrive over the years, a positive mental and emotional framework, the constant choice of faith over fear, is what will get you there.

Can You Build a Support Structure around Yourself?

Even as your ministry bears fruit, even as God's plan finds new shapes, even as you commission people to go out in ministry—even as you do all these things, you'll still need to plan for the marathon. It's important to have a tangible plan for personal maintenance. We are human, and there are simply too many obstructions to keep us from being all that we wish to be for God's kingdom.

One essential move is to allow others to partner with you, to hold you accountable. Some pastors are overseen by denominational boards or by accountability boards made up of other pastors in different cities. That's okay at the beginning, but you need to be moving toward setting up accountability within your own church. Some pastors really have no accountability system. I believe that every pastor should have some form of accountability from within the church. The pastor and staff need the leeway to make ongoing decisions, but the pastor also must receive encouragement and oversight from people qualified to doctrinally evaluate his teaching, to check in on his family, and to meet other needs.

At West Ridge Church the elder team has one employee—the senior pastor. They love me, strengthen me, and also ask me the tough questions. Leadership can be lonely, and I welcome the opportunity to have good people keeping me company on the front line. I tell them, "You guys are the guardrails, not the guard dogs, right?" They laugh, but they'll dog me if they have to, if they find out that I'm not taking care of my health, or if I'm not there for my family as much as I should be, or if I spread myself too thin in ministry. I can thrive because God has lifted up some mighty men, just like David's mighty men, to help me.

I've also created an informal network of pastors, friends, and mentors whose opinions I value. I talk to them regularly, get their take on big decisions, and count on them to be honest with me. Too many pastors become insulated, surrounded with people who would never question their judgment. As you plant a church, build in your guardrails from the very beginning.

You'll need to build margin into your life too. Author Richard A. Swensen defines margin as "the space that once existed between ourselves and our limits." How often are you overloaded? I believe that most church planters are overloaded, and almost by necessity. God speaks to us in the margins. He has always spoken to me when I've taken the time to go somewhere, sit prayerfully with my journal, and listen.

Look at the margin on this page—the white space near the edge. You need white space in your life, emptiness and quietness in which God can say something new to you. Your family needs margin. Your marriage needs margin. You can survive without it, but believe me, you'll never thrive in the field of ministry without it. Lack of margin will age you prematurely. It will create anxiety, which in turn will destroy your health and trouble your soul. If you have a maintenance plan for your car, your home, even your computer, why not for the life and career God has given you?

We remind ourselves that what we are giving our lives to is the most important cause on earth and that it is an honor that God chose us to help build his church! He could have asked anyone, but he asked us. Having other pastors and pastors' wives in our life who are passionate about the ministry has also helped us thrive. They are a lifeline during those tough seasons.

— Bil and Jessica Cornelius,
Bay Area Fellowship, Corpus Christie, TX

Can You Fully Rest in the Love of Christ?

During my early years of ministry, I would drive from my little township of Pemberton down to Long Beach Island for a special purpose. I wanted to meet with another of my mentors, Dr. Al Oldham, who was then the director of Harvey Cedars Bible Conference in New Jersey. I would sit at a picnic table with Dr. Oldham and talk with him about the difficulties of ministry and how lonely I was at the time. He was loving, patient, and encouraging.

I sat with him again this past summer. I'm at midlife, he's eighty-four, and the world has changed over time more than either of us. I wasn't griping so much now; I was more interested in listening than talking. I knew I might not see Dr. O again. You don't replace that kind of resource.

I looked at him and said, "Dr. O, looking back at your life, what is the greatest lesson that God has taught you?"

He smiled. "You know, Brian, I used to be such a staunch defender of Reformed doctrine. I could get into all the details of divine election and dissect any argument. Now I'm older, I'm in a battle with cancer, and I can honestly tell you that the one great truth I've learned is that God loves me."

I knew what he meant. One of the most brilliant theologians of the twentieth century was Karl Barth. Toward the end of his life, he faced a similar question. Barth was asked how he would summarize the millions of words he had published in his lifetime. He replied, "Jesus loves me, this I know, for the Bible tells me so."

I no longer burn to be the greatest preacher alive, though I want to be as effective as I can. I don't lie awake comparing myself with others in this category or that, and I've accepted that I have weaknesses and will always have them. I'm at peace, and it's because I've come to grips with the fact that God loves me and that his acceptance is all that really matters. When I turn out the light at the end of a day, I can go to sleep, regardless of whether every problem in my ministry has been hammered out. It is well with my soul because Jesus is enough.

It's obvious. It shouldn't even have to be said. How could anyone spend any time at all in the New Testament and not realize the truth that we are completely and eternally reconciled with God in Christ? And yet I know so many Christian leaders who can't walk before their people and demonstrate a living model of absolute rest in Christ. I have to admit, I'm still working on it myself.

If all my sins are truly forgiven; if I face an eternity in the presence of God, where every tear will be dried and there will be no more pain or sorrow; if to live is Christ and to die is gain, as Paul tells us, then why should I worry? I should be able to thrive. If the very best I can do is to grimly hang on and survive, what's the point? How am I different from someone who has never heard the news about Jesus Christ? Why should that nonbeliever find anything I say compelling?

This life should be more than a grim struggle with principalities and powers. It should be a deep thrill and an ultimate joy, even with all its challenges. Do you have what it takes to endure, to blossom, to thrive?

How do you thrive, not just survive, in ministry?

Being in ministry can be one of the most taxing callings on anyone's life. To say that being on pastoral staff at a church is a 24/7 commitment would be one of the great understatements of the century. With hospital visits, marriage counseling, funerals, weddings, sermon preparation, ministry planning, outreach efforts, and so on, it is not difficult to understand why someone who is simply trying to survive one day at a time would burn out quickly in ministry. However, there is an antidote to this very real challenge. The answer is found in our priorities. What's really important? The only way to thrive in ministry is to focus on those areas of life and ministry that are the most important and have the most impact. In our personal lives, it's our relationship and walk with God and our relationship with our family. God and family always come first. In ministry, it's all about life change. You will find great joy and accomplishment when you focus on the marriage that has been pulled from the brink of disaster because of your ministry, the man who has walked away from alcoholism or drug addiction, the teenager who just walked down the aisle in your worship service to accept Christ, or the precious lady you were able to pray with just before she slipped into heaven. Sure, ministry is tough. Sure, the hours are long. Sure, the stress can be overwhelming. But when in the throes of stress and discouragement you once again picture the faces of those you've helped, it will always give you the extra encouragement you need to make it through the day. Paul told us in 1 Corinthians 9:25, "They do it to get a crown that will not last, but we do it to get a crown that will last forever." We serve for the eternal crown, not the ones that can be trashed by the trials of this world. It's all about life change. Remember that — and you will thrive!

— Jonathan and Shari Falwell,
Thomas Road Baptist Church, Lynchburg, VA

CHAPTER 12

WHEN DOES IT BECOME TOO PERSONAL?

Do you need an exit strategy?

Jeff and Christy Murphy have been our close friends since college years. They also planted one of the first churches that West Ridge helped to launch. It opened in Sugar Hill, Georgia, in 2002 — and closed five years later, leaving our friends devastated spiritually, emotionally, and even financially.

Anyone who meets Jeff and Christy would be able to tell you after five minutes, "Oh, yeah — those two are going to be a huge success." And it wouldn't matter what field you were talking about. Both of them are gifted, warm, energetic, charismatic, and highly articulate. In college, Jeff was known as a "party waiting to happen." Christy is just as remarkable, with her own set of talents.

The Sugar Hill church started well. Jeff and Christy made all the right moves, and West Ridge offered as much support as we could. Staff were hired, and a school cafeteria was quickly found for holding the services. Every time we talked to Jeff, it seemed he had led new people to Christ — workout buddies, mountain bike buddies — and plugged them into the church.

But something wasn't right. The momentum just ran out. Nearly all the promising young workout buddies got job transfers and moved to other states. The executive pastor retired. Two steps forward, three steps back. The Murphys believed in the church, and they had sunk everything they had into it. They had raised support, liquidated their savings account, sold off stocks, and done everything they could to keep staff salaries paid — but the finances were hemorrhaging.

The odd thing is that Jeff and Christy both felt God tugging their hearts toward the city of Columbus, Georgia. *What about Sugar Hill, Lord?* God was silent on the current church. Jeff had been a youth pastor in Columbus, and the couple's first child was born there. Jeff was there occasionally to perform a wedding or visit a friend, and he couldn't escape the impression that God had something for him there — even as the Sugar Hill church was clearly on life support.

Eventually the Murphys met with their leaders and discussed options. "We feel God leading us to leave," Jeff told them, "but we want to help you find a new lead pastor for Sugar Hill."

The leaders shocked them. They said that if the Murphys left, eighty to ninety percent of them would most likely go to other churches rather than hang around through a leadership transition. There was no real interest in keeping the church plant alive; for them, the church wasn't as tangible as it would have seemed if they'd had their own building. Actually, land had been reserved for one — and the Murphys were left financially responsible for it. The Murphys were going to obey God, but that meant seeing their beloved Sugar Hill plant fizzle.

For Jeff, this meant admitting he had given five years of his life to something that didn't work. He had always carried the philosophy of making things happen by outworking the competition. Closing a church was against every impulse the couple had. "It's like shooting your own child," Jeff said, expressing just how raw his emotions were. Christie felt as if it was flatly unbiblical to close a church. Their children were unhappy about things too.

But there was really no choice. Jeff's last sermon was a practical one, telling his friends how to go about finding another church. The tears flowed down his cheeks as he spoke.

The Murphys stayed in the Atlanta area for a full year after the church shut down. He still had to show up to mow the lawn of the old office space. Cars would pass by, and Jeff would think, "Well, here's the successful preacher, mowing the grass that is all that's left of his work." He also presided over a big "fire sale" for other planters and church administrators looking for sound equipment, children's stuff, and three enclosed trailers that had been purchased: the sum total of their ministry, now a garage sale.

For a year and a half the Murphys dealt with their pain, their sense of failure, their questions about God and his providence. They were burned out, but they decided to ride out the storm and take part in a church-planting residency program for a year. They lived on five hundred dollars per month and were ready to move on to something else, even if that meant serving cones in an ice cream parlor and saying, "God loves you."

Jeff's thoughts were, *I'm the guy that shut a church down. I'm the stupid and broken guy who let down God.*

But he began to hear another—powerful—voice, saying, *No. I'm the one who shut the church down. You let down nobody. It's not always about you; you're just part of a greater story that you can't see ahead of you. What the two of you need for right now is to heal.*

Jeff and Christy heard God's voice. Strange!—they hadn't even realized their need for healing. What they came to understand was that God is the one who grows a church. If he had wanted it to survive, it would have survived. It was all part of another story God was writing. (There is always a story behind the story, and a plot line in that story is Jeff and Christy's need to be *stripped down*. They were so gifted that they depended on their own talents. They were so devoted to one another that they leaned on one another. What God wanted was for them to depend upon *him*, to lean solely on *him*. They could not learn that lesson without coming to the end of themselves.)

Jeff says, "The amazing thing is that I can be honest now. I always thought I was honest and transparent, but until you're broken, there's that part of you that is afraid people are going to find you out; they're going to see that you don't have it as together as what you present.

"Christy and I no longer live in fear for our reputations. We love people just as much, but we're freed up to be honest, because we know that we can do nothing at all without the power of God. We're liberated from that burden of performance, but it's a lesson you can learn only through pain."

Christy says something really profound: "None of us would ever choose the road that God has for us. But it's the best road for us to walk. He has to do what it takes to get us on it, despite ourselves."

In 2009, Jeff and Christy launched a new church in Columbus, Georgia. They did exactly what they had done at Sugar Hill. But this time God was writing the story — the whole story. Six hundred were there on the first Sunday. A thousand people attend each week now, only three years in.

I'm one of the overseers for Jeff, and Amy and I will tell you this: We've known Jeff and Christy for many years, but the change in them is remarkable. God has prepared them to do an amazing work. He had to get personal, things had to get painful, but they'll tell you that it's been more than worth every tear.

Sheep Bite

Jeff and Christie always loved God. They had given their lives and everything they had to help build his church, so that his people could come to know him.

But it's not always easy. Sometimes things just don't work, for reasons only God knows. For another thing, the sheep bite.

We are called to shepherd people, but sometimes sheep have surprisingly sharp teeth. And the danger is that, even when we love the Lord and live in the power of his Spirit, we retain a little residue from negative confrontations. That residue builds up.

When we're not careful, it spills out at all kinds of times.

Most church planters learn how to suppress their anger — if they didn't, they wouldn't last too long. But suppressed anger doesn't simply go away. It stays inside until it finds some kind of escape valve. Counselors will tell you that eventually it comes out *passive-aggressively.* That is, it becomes a kind of "stealth anger" that expresses itself indirectly toward people who didn't even cause it in the first place. For example, a teenager who is angry but isn't allowed to express her anger may later start failing classes even though she's capable of passing them. She might act out in some other way.

Whether your anger tends to be direct or passive, you need to deal with it as quickly as it comes. This is why the Bible tells us, " 'In your anger do not sin': Do not let the sun go down while you are still angry" (Eph. 4:26).

Some pastors don't handle their emotions wisely, and it begins to accumulate. Soon they find themselves venting, without really knowing why. Maybe they have been hurt or misunderstood. They may have experienced discouragement, disappointment, or loneliness that they have never known before. *Sometimes pastors and their wives know so much personal and confidential information about people they are trying to help that they feel overwhelmed.* They begin to file away names in their minds — names of people with whom they've clashed. They don't realize they've created an enemies list, while the Bible teaches us to deal with all people with grace, love, and mercy. We don't have the power to do that, of course — we have to love people through God's Spirit.

Angry, hurt pastors can become cynical pastors, and it shows. Friends and family struggle to understand how it happened. What happened is that at some point, this work became too personal.

We've held throughout this book that nothing could be more

up close and personal than church planting. But there's a difference between taking it personally and taking it so personally that it becomes toxic; so personally that you begin to lose your effectiveness. So, then, when does church planting become too personal? It becomes too personal when you lose sight of the fact that it is God's church. He will take full credit for the victories and full responsibility for the challenges.

It's possible to come to a place where you, the fisher of men

When people leave our churches, when they criticize our leadership or budget decisions, when they question our motives, our tendency is to take it personally. We can't avoid some type of personal feelings. We wouldn't be compassionate, loving leaders if it didn't hurt to some degree. This will always feel personal. However, the problem increases when one word is added — the word *too*. The danger is in taking it "too" personal. Unfortunately, I have done this "too" many times.

When we take things too personally, we are in essence making their decisions and criticisms about us. We forget that many people make decisions and judgments completely apart from us and that often their actions come from their own past and current pain. Also, the church belongs to Christ (even if we planted it), so when we take things too personally, we take ownership of the church instead of stewardship of the church. This makes us as spiritually unhealthy as those who are leaving and criticizing.

I try to remember that it's okay that it hurts, but not okay to take it too personally. The people are not really leaving me. I don't need to feel rejection when I know in my heart that this church is not about me, but it's about Christ. One day my wife, Donna, so wisely reminded me, "Hey, don't take it so personally. Since when was this thing ever about you?" Gotta love her.

— Tommy and Donna Politz,
Hillside Christian Church, Amarillo, TX

and women, find yourself thinking, "I don't even particularly like people anymore. I don't like the things they say. I don't like the things they do. I don't like the way they make me feel."

It's even possible for a pastor to become just a little paranoid, thinking there is an enemy behind every rock; wondering who is whispering about him; avoiding people when he sees them; suspecting that some little group is going to form a faction.

Transformation

If you want to observe some vintage emotion, open to the center of your Bible. There's a book in there called Psalms with some pretty devastating confessions of pain. Sometimes the psalms are addressed toward other people, sometimes toward self, sometimes even toward God. David, a very emotional and very gifted human being, wrote a number of these psalms. He knew what it was like to have people — a king, or even his own son — conspiring against him. He also understood what would happen when he didn't control his passion.

So he brought his anger and hurt to God, in all its ugliness, and dumped it at the foot of the throne. The wonderful irony is that God saw fit to include it in his inspired Word! One of the countless wonderful things about the Bible is that it's a fully divine book, yet it's also so wise and so real in the humanity it contains. The message of those psalms is that God understands you; he doesn't condemn you.

I'm thankful to the bottom of my soul that Jesus never became fed up with the people he was sent to save. He forgave the very ones who nailed him to the cross. If he could do that, maybe I could trust God to help me be merciful toward difficult people, with all their shortcomings — even when they're not merciful toward me.

Even so, we want this book to be as realistic as it can possibly be. Having recognized that we have such spiritual resources to draw upon — the power of the Holy Spirit, the listening ears of loving friends — we want to recognize that there will be some people for whom this journey simply becomes too personal.

If you find that it has become too personal for you, don't feel as though you have let God or people down if you feel that you need to walk away, for your emotional health, to protect your family or marriage, or for some other reason. There are people and situations when it's surely the right thing to do, and if this is the case, we know that our God is sovereign, that no turn of events surprises him, and that he has another bright destiny for you. Claim Jeremiah 29:11: " 'I know the plans I have for you,' declares the LORD, 'plans to prosper you and not to harm you, plans to give you hope and a future.' "

A Vision for Tomorrow

Some mornings I wake up, and it hits me: *This is amazing — this life!*

As of 2012, there are now seven billion people on this planet. Do you know how many of them God is pursuing? Seven billion! He loves every single one of them with a passion so deep we can't

> When people leave our church, the first thing I (Ike) think is, I must have screwed up, so I say, "God, show me if I've done something wrong." If I have, then I apologize, but if not, then I have to deal with not letting a root of bitterness get into my heart. When this root is mentioned in the Bible, it is referring to a particular kind of root that makes a dye or a stain. If you allow a root of bitterness, it will color your relationships and stain the way you look at the world.
>
> — Ike and Robin Reighard,
> Piedmont Baptist Church, Marietta, Georgia

begin to imagine it. He sent his son Jesus, who became flesh and offered himself on the cross because he dearly loves those seven billion, along with everyone else who has ever walked on this planet. As a parent loves a child, so he loves each one of them.

And Jesus is calling us — you and me — to work with him, to be part of a heaven-and-earth partnership to reach all of those people. This entire life, from womb to tomb, is a rescue mission. We know that this rescue mission is the most important thing in the world, that it is worthy of our lives, and that it is very personal to a very relational God.

That is why church planting is so thrilling! To us it is the greatest day-to-day, face-to-face adventure imaginable. I understand climbing Mount Everest would be thrilling. I can imagine that being an astronaut on the space station would be unforgettable. But seeing souls come to trust Christ is vastly, *unimaginably* greater because the most humble, most ordinary human beings — the souls that you and I lead to Christ — *those people are* eternal, and you and I have played a role in helping to change their eternal destination.

You and I have just partnered with God to enlarge the size of heaven.

Did you take that in?

When we consider these things, we have a renewed sense of just how much it is *not* about us. Our God is so magnificently awesome that it *absolutely* must be *completely* about him.

Amy and I have a vision that someday, at the end of our lives, our personalities won't have mattered much, but like mirrors, we will have reflected the fact that it was all about Jesus.

Because to him, it's *personal*.

We hope it will be personal for you, too.

ACKNOWLEDGMENTS

Thank you to the wonderful people of West Ridge Church who have courageously walked this personal journey with us. We are so honored to serve you and to call you our family.

Thank you to Steve and Christie Veale, Paul and Angela Richardson, and Dave and Chris Cole. You believed that God was at work in northwest Atlanta, and you took a life-changing journey with us. You will always have a special place in our hearts.

Thank you to our core group for believing in us and faithfully serving along side of us for fifteen years. You are special indeed!

To the amazing staff, elders, and leadership team of West Ridge, thank you for partnering with us. We love doing ministry and life with you!

Thank you to our mentors—Dave and Becky Adams, Doug and Jane Randlett, John and Carolyn Hibbard, Bob and Doris English, Johnny and Janet Hunt, Ike and Robin Reighard, and Jerry and Macel Falwell—for your investment in our lives, our marriage, and our ministry.

To Michael and Jenniffer Marblestone, Matt and Chris Wilmington, and Tommy and Donna Politz, thank you for your friendship through the years, especially over the past year as we wrote this book.

To the gracious church-planting couples that we interviewed, thank you for being so transparent and contributing to this book.

To church planters and their spouses and kids, thank you for answering God's call. Church planting is kingdom work, and we are all in this together.

Thank you to Brian's assistant, Judy Marshall, for helping us to coordinate our crazy schedules so we could write together. Thank you to Jim Akins, our original church planting guru, for helping us with research. And to Dan Schroeter and Kevin Bloye for investing some early editing efforts into this book.

To our brothers and sisters, Kathryn and Darren, Donna and Jonathan, Dave and Kerry, Kevin and Dawn and Jonathan. Thank you not only for being family, but for being our closest friends.

Thank you to Exponential (Todd Wilson and Terry Saliba) and Leadership Network for giving us this opportunity. Thank you to Zondervan (Ryan Pazdur, Andrew Rogers, and Jim Ruark) for being so great to work with. Thank you to Mark Sweeney for being a wonderful consultant throughout this project.

To the LAUNCH Church Planting Network, our board members, and Mac and Cindy Lake, thank you for partnering with us to plant healthy churches that lead strong!

To Andy Stanley, thank you for your investment in our lives and the lives of other leaders, for personally being a wise mentor and a great listener, and for writing the foreword for our book.

And especially, to our collaborator, Rob Suggs, we have laughed and cried together. We have also eaten a lot of frozen yogurt together over the past year. Thank you for having a heart for church planting. We could not have written this book without you!

The interest in church planting has grown significantly in recent years. The need for new churches has never been greater. At the same time, the number of models and approaches is expanding. To address the unique opportunities of churches in this landscape, Exponential Network, in partnership with Leadership Network and Zondervan, launched the *Exponential Series* in 2010.

Books in this series:

- Tell the reproducing church story
- Celebrate the diversity of models and approaches God is using to reproduce healthy congregations
- Highlight the innovative and pioneering practices of healthy reproducing churches
- Equip, inspire, and challenge Kingdom-minded leaders with the tools they need in their journey of becoming reproducing church leaders

Exponential exists to attract, inspire, and equip Kingdom-minded leaders to engage in a movement of high-impact, reproducing churches. We provide a national voice for this movement through the Exponential Conference, the Exponential Initiative, Exponential Venture, and the Exponential Series.

Leadership Network exists to accelerate the impact of 100X leaders. Believing that meaningful conversations and strategic connections can change the world, we seek to help leaders navigate the future by exploring new ideas and finding application for each unique context.

For more information about the *Exponential Series*, go to:

www.exponentialseries.com